50 plus one

Fun Things to Do with Kids During Summer

by
Ann Kepler

Information to Encourage Achievement

1261 West Glenlake
Chicago, IL 60660
www.encouragementpress.com

ISBN13: 978-1-933766-10-2   ISBN10: 1-933766-10-7

This product is not intended to provide legal or financial advice or substitute for the advice of an attorney or advisor.

10 9 8 7 6 5 4 3 2 1
♻ printed on recycled paper

© 2007 Encouragement Press, LLC
1261 West Glenlake
Chicago, IL 60660

Special discounts on bulk quantities of Encouragement Press books and products are available to corporations, professional associations and other organizations. For details, contact our Special Sales Department at 1.253.303.0033.

About the Author

Ann Kepler is the author of *Children's Medicine: A Guide for Parents* and The American Medical Association's *Family Medical Guide to Alternative and Conventional Treatments* as well as a dozen other books ranging from lifestyle to technical subjects. She teaches writing and has received numerous academic, professional and civic honors. When she is not writing or teaching, she devises and participates in games and activities with the preschoolers and young children in her family.

Acknowledgements

Special thanks…and cheers to the following:

Carol Klein

Table of Contents

The Entire Family

Introduction

"I'm bored. There's nothing to do."

How many times have you heard your kids say that at the beginning of what promises to be a very long day?

Whether or not you are at home with the kids all day or at work wondering what they are doing while you are away, you may feel hard pressed to find something to occupy the kids during the day. Each year's school summer vacation, especially, seems to stretch endlessly into the future. While you may have pleasant memories of playing outside by yourself all day during the summer–you can still hear your parents' admonition, "Don't slam the screen door" on your trips in and out of the house–this may not be an option today. For various reasons, you may want to select and supervise your children's activities and this requires some advance planning on your part.

This is the book to help you do just that.

This book lists 50 plus one activities that you can do with your children during that endless summer vacation, school holidays, snow days, weekends or long empty afternoons. You will find a range of activities from those suitable for the preschooler level to those more appropriate for older children. Some activities can be intergenerational, meaning that older children can help younger children or adults can either participate or supervise. You will want to adapt each activity to the needs and skill levels of all the participants.

We have organized the activities in this book by type to help you find ones that appeal to you or are suitable for your situation on any given day. There are indoor activities, which include, among other projects, crafts, board games, reading, music-making, drama presentations and make-believe adventures. Make-believe adventures can also move outside to join such fun pursuits as sports, nature hunts, outdoor water play, and running games. We have also included suggestions about stocking supplies and remaining prepared.

Many people think that the work of children is play, so almost any play activity can be educational. That is why you will find a definite educational slant to many of the exercises described in this book. For example, a child can learn math by measuring recipe ingredients in the kitchen. Or learn to think sequentially while following instructions to repair a toy or household object. Or practice safety while working with tools. There are both simple recipes for preparing dishes and instructions for constructing playthings. These kinds of experiences are included here in an effort to reinforce learning in a realistic, hands-on manner. Plus, the child will be learning life skills and helping out at the same time.

Not all learning or fun takes place at home, so there is a section in this book on excursions. Some excursions require money, while others require time. Still others require neither. Regardless of the time or the money, however, excursions do require access. Therefore, the information here is general—how to get the most out of a museum trip or a day at the beach or a visit to a park, for example—since not everyone has access to these sites. Even so, everyone may find the tips on whiling away time while en route helpful. To help you learn more about these activities and topics, we are including additional resources throughout the book. We may refer you to a Website or cite a book or another reference. We are doing this to give you a broader idea of what you can do to adapt ideas to meet the needs of your kids and to tailor activities to your own situation. The goal is to foster fun while encouraging interaction among everyone in your family. We hope this will enable you to enjoy your time together.

So make some room on your shelf of reference books. You will want to grab this book the next time you hear,

"There's nothing to do. I am so bo-o-ored."

Ann Kepler

plus one

Fun, Educational & Healthy Alternatives to Computers & TV

I am bored. There is nothing to do.

These phrases used to be reoccurring complaints heard on long days in the summer. Today, however, kids often retreat to their computers and electronic games–or the TV–to while away their spare hours.

What about those days that are sunny and balmy? When the weather is neither too hot nor too cool and the day beckons everyone to spend time outdoors? The kids remain in front of the computer or the TV.

Computers and Electronic Games–Good or Bad?

Is this good or bad? It can be either. There are advantages to encouraging your child to become computer-proficient. Playing on computers or electronic games can be educational. Both encourage hand-eye coordination and help young children learn shapes, colors, numbers and letters. Beginner computer programs designed for children are vocabulary builders. In addition, computers can teach the relationship between cause and effect; when a child presses a key on the keyboard, something happens on the screen.

Yet too much time in front of a computer screen during the first 3 years of a child's life may not be a good idea. During their first 3 years, kids build the foundation for their own creativity and develop motor skills by interacting with other people and their environment. Computers or electronic games do not require interaction with other people, so young children play in isolation without learning how to play with other children or to respond to their surroundings. Also, there may be a delay in language development since kids do not need to express their ideas or needs in words. Merely by pushing a key, their needs are met.

Furthermore, while many educators acknowledge the benefits of computers and electronic games, they believe that children can develop the same skills through old-fashioned activities, such as playing with blocks and other toys or reading books.

A Question of Health

Spending a great deal of time at a computer or in front of the TV is not just a matter of delayed intellectual growth. There is also a question of physical growth and health. Today more children than ever are overweight, even obese, which can be attributed to lack of physical activity. Allowing your children to spend a disproportionate amount of time sitting in front of the computer or the TV rather than participating in games and activities that exercise their bodies can lead to health risks, both now and later in life. This is particularly true if a child develops a pattern or habit of inactivity that may continue through the teen years and into adulthood. Childhood obesity has been defined as a body weight 20 percent over the recommended weight for height, and recent research indicates that 11 percent of children between the ages of 6 and 11 and 14 percent of teens between the ages of 12 and 17 meet this definition. If allowed to continue, this kind of body weight can lead to chronic conditions including heart disease, high blood pressure and diabetes. Yes, type 2 adult onset diabetes is becoming common among children.

Fitness

Fitness has also declined among children. This can lead not only to obesity and its problems but also to physical development setbacks. Children of all ages need to learn fundamental motor skills as well as develop endurance, muscular strength and flexibility. They need to establish the habit of activity from an early age and to experience the pleasure of achieving new physical skills as they grow and mature.

How can you encourage fitness? By striving to incorporate at least 30 minutes–60 minutes is better for kids–of vigorous activity into your child's schedule each day. This may sound silly to those of you with active, rambunctious kids, but many families do need to establish this kind of schedule. This does not have to be regimented; walking, bicycling, playing running games or even helping with household and yard chores may fulfill the goal. And it does not have to occur at one time; five 10-minute periods scattering throughout the day is also beneficial. Most of all, instilling a positive attitude about the need for daily physical exercise is essential. You can do that by setting an example if you find that you should be more physically active each day.

One handy reference is the MyActivity Pyramid (see Resources at the end of this chapter), which includes guidelines for physical activity for children between the ages of 6 and 11. Developed by the University of Missouri-Columbia Extension health educators, the pyramid is fashioned on the U.S. Department of Agriculture's MyPyramid food guide. The pyramid is built of various levels that show what kind of and how much activity kids need. The widest level at the base of the pyramid recommends everyday activities–the ones the kids should participate in the most. These include riding a bike to school, playground and recess games and daily chores. The next level recommends vigorous activities that kids need between three to five times a week, such as sports, running or rollerblading. The third level from the bottom of the pyramid suggests doing activities that promote flexibility and strength at least twice a week. These include martial arts, pushups and yoga. The very top of the pyramid, taking up the least amount of space, lists inactive endeavors, such as playing computer games or watching TV. This section of the pyramid suggests that computer games and TV be limited to 2 or fewer hours per day.

Getting Started

Now that you have seen the disadvantages of prolonged computer and TV activities and the health dvantages of physical activity, what can you do to help your kids while away the summer days while encouraging intellectual and physical growth and development? Remember, unless your kids are enrolled in a sports or camp program, they will not have the benefit of the school's physical education program during the summer vacation.

The best solution is probably the middle road: Taking advantage of the benefits of the computer and electronic toys while encouraging play with old-fashioned toys and games that require a child's imagination and creativity and promote physical fitness and exercise. Remember, too, that over the summer vacation, many kids may forget some basic skills they acquired during the school year, so you want to plan activities that can help maintain skill levels. Summer vacation does not have to be a vacation from retaining knowledge accumulated during the school year.

It will take some planning on your part, but it is possible to put together a summer plan that will keep the kids busy yet learning, industrious yet challenged. You can start by referring to the MyActivity Pyramid for ideas and a balanced program of exercise. You can plan to include activities that require supervision (learning to cook or water sports) or allow free rein for the participants (traditional outdoor games such as tag). You can include learning games (yes, there are learning games that are not computer-based, such as games about counting or spelling), craft activities (papier-mâché, knitting or mobiles) or artistic endeavors (puppet shows, collages or sidewalk art). And you can include activities that involve the entire family (bike riding, excursions or building a family tree).

Planning is important because in today's world a parent has to consider not only each child's needs but also the environment. There are issues of safety and security as well as parental time. If you are a working parent, you may have to alter your plans to accommodate the babysitter or caregiver's time and abilities. Some activities cost money; others are free or require only ingenuity. All of these factors have to be considered when you are building a summer plan of activities.

Gone are the days of a generation or more ago when mothers simply ordered the kids to go outside and play. Now you have to factor in time, schedules, safety and location. And you must not forget fun. Your plan of activities should not look like a list of chores. It should include activities that stimulate wholehearted participation, and it should allow some time for just sitting around and thinking—perhaps contemplating clouds while lying in the grass. You should put together a plan of summer fun and learning that is seamless enough to become a part of a daily routine that is not overscheduled or forced. Otherwise, it will probably not work.

And do not become upset if every now and then you simply have to tell your kids to go find something to do and get some fresh air. Your kids might surprise you with their ingenuity in finding something to do on their own. Most kids—especially older kids—enjoy taking control of their time and can occupy themselves for a period of time. The key is to set up a standard of meaningful activity without turning to the computer or the TV. If you show your kids that they can have fun without automatically sitting down at the computer or in front of the TV, they will usually opt to find something to do that does not require electronic equipment.

Your goal is a fun, yet educational, summer. Since learning can be fun, these two objectives complement each other. Quiet games, active games, learning games and family games all contribute to this goal. You will be doing your kids a favor—developing both intellectual skills and physical fitness and strength—by turning off the computer and the TV and encouraging other types of activities. You and your kids have nothing to lose and much to gain by returning to those days when summer fun meant using mind and body to learn and play.

Resources

http://muextension.missouri.edu/explore/hesguide/foodnut/n00386.htm

This Website illustrates the MyActivity Pyramid and offers specific suggestions for appropriate activities for each level of the pyramid. It is a good planning resource.

www.kidsource.com/kidsource/content4/promote.phyed.html

This Website discusses the needs of various types of activities for children and the consequences of a sedentary lifestyle.

1
Learning to Cook

Kids of all ages can benefit from spending time in the kitchen because easy-to-understand recipes teach aptitudes such as basic math skills, reading comprehension and creative problem solving. In addition, learning how to follow directions is an important life skill for success in school and in later life.

To use cooking as a tool for teaching, begin with simple fractions: Cut a banana or a sandwich into several equal parts. Then move on to more complex ideas such as metric measurements, proportions and basic chemistry. Even your toddler can learn by playing in the cupboards with the pots and pans; size and shape concepts lay the foundation for basic math skills. Ignore the mess and let them explore while you supervise for safety.

Starting Out

Children of any age can work in the kitchen with an adult present, so long as the recipes are modified accordingly. Use your judgment to decide when your child is ready to attempt a new challenge and be right there for the results. Here are some tips:

- Young chefs may be more likely to try a food or a dish if they help prepare it. Even very young children–between the ages of 2 and 6–like to break eggs, tear up spinach or lettuce, knead bread or mash food. Just be certain they wash their hands before and after handling food, especially raw eggs.
- Look for no-cook recipes that do not call for knives, stovetops or ovens for older children who are just learning to cook and are not yet proficient in the kitchen.
- Add only one new lesson at a time even after a child begins to gain confidence in the kitchen. Do not introduce the vegetable peeler or a new cooking technique, for example, on the same day you use the blender for the first time.
- Allow any child that has mastered reading, regardless of age, to take control of the recipe card. This will help her quickly learn the abbreviations for

kitchen terms and get a firm grip on measurements and fractions. Allow the child to read each item, retrieve it and then decide which measurement container to use; request that the child show you before pouring it into the mixture or batter.

- When your child has mastered the recipe card and can make a recipe independently, practice doubling the recipe or halving it. This is a great way to build math skills.
- Allow your child to clean up when she finishes a recipe. Do not get into the habit of having many hands cutting, chopping and stirring only to be left with the task of having to clean up after your child.

Important Safety Precautions

Taking the following precautions can help prevent mishaps and injury in the kitchen:

- Turn handles inward so pots and pans will not be pulled off or knocked off the stove.
- Dress appropriately for cooking by wearing short or tight-fitting sleeves when cooking and using caution when working near heat sources. Avoid reaching over the stove or behind the stovetop by storing items you use in more safely accessible locations.
- Keep young children away from appliances when cooking. Enforce a kid-free zone around the stove and teach youngsters not to play in that area. If you allow older children to cook, supervise them closely while teaching them safe cooking practices.
- Use caution with electrical appliances. Plug only one appliance into an outlet at a time and repair appliances with frayed or cracked cords before using them. Be extra careful when working around water and be sure to teach your child never to stand in water or near it when using electrical appliances.
- Never allow a child in the kitchen when you are using a deep fryer or heating oil in a frying pan. We have all been splashed with popping oil, but it is even more dangerous for a child who is at or below eye level of this dangerous, hot liquid. Always heat oil slowly and keep the pan lid close at hand to guard against splattering grease.
- Learn how to deal with a fire. If a fire is confined to a pan on top of the stove, slide the lid across the pan and leave it there. Do not attempt to move the pan outdoors because you may burn yourself or spread the fire. Never throw water or flour on a burning pan. Water will spread the flames and flour will actually explode!

To avoid foodborne illness, wash hands and clean food preparation surfaces frequently. Insist that your children follow the same rules. If you or your kids handle raw meat or poultry, wash your hands and your children's hands afterward. Separate raw, cooked and ready-to-eat foods whenever you are shopping for food, preparing food or storing food.

Basic Cooking Techniques

Sometimes we grow so comfortable with something we have done for years that we forget it once may have been difficult or frustrating for us. Measuring ingredients for a recipe is one of those tasks.

You should teach your children the proper way to measure ingredients in order to get the desired results. Tossing in an extra pinch of this and a sprinkle of that comes with years of practice and many experimental failures along the way. Without a firm understanding of measurement, this talent may never develop.

Just in case you have forgotten your basic home economics course, here are guidelines for properly measuring ingredients:

Solids Versus Liquids

There is a difference between solid and liquid measuring containers. The solid measuring cups are the stackable containers that come in various sizes. The liquid container is the large measuring cup with lined increments printed up the side. The only way to get an exact measurement with either type of ingredient is to use the proper container.

Solids

Dry ingredients should be spooned into the measuring container while holding the measuring cup over the bag or canister you are using. Using flour as an example, place the cup over the open bag so any overflow falls back into the bag. Spoon the flour into the cup until it heaps over the top. Take a flat-edged instrument, such as a butter knife, and scrape across the lip of the measuring cup to create a perfectly even, completely filled cup. Measuring spoons should be filled in the same manner. Do not forget to teach that brown sugar needs to be firmly packed.

Liquids

Liquid should be poured into a cup while the cup is exactly at eye level. You can demonstrate the importance of this by filling a container while standing above it. Once it is filled to a particular level, have your child bring it to eye level to see how close the measured amount is to your goal. Measuring spoons should be filled right to the top without any spillover.

Ingredients and Supplies to Keep on Hand

When children are just starting to cook, it is important for them to develop basic mixing skills and to respect kitchen tools. Use plastic or metal bowls that will not break, teach respect for sharp knives and avoid using electrical appliances. To give your child a chance to practice cutting, let her practice with a nonserrated butter knife on soft foods like bananas and ripe pears. Once you are comfortable with her technique, move on to a sharper knife. Children from the ages of 6 and older who show promise may begin to use paring knives whose blades are no longer than their hands. Watch carefully to make sure that as your child holds down the food she's cutting, that she curls her fingers under so as not to expose her fingertips. Do not purposely dull a knife, thinking that it will be safer.

A similar principle of safety applies to pans on the stove. You should begin with recipes that require mixing, spreading and spooning but no heat. As you progress toward dishes that call for use of the stove or oven, ask your child to observe you carefully, then have her assist you as you deem appropriate.

Good ingredients for no-cook recipes include peanut butter, yogurt, honey, shredded coconut, grated cheese, frozen juices, fresh and frozen fruits, cream cheese, raisins and chocolate chips. The Internet and your local public library have cookbooks with no-cook recipes designed specifically with children in mind.

Since eating is something we all need to do every day, involving your children can make cooking fun, strengthen family bonds and help your children learn while developing a practical skill. It is never too early to say, bon appétit!

There is no better place to teach counting and money skills than in a grocery store. Take your kids along when you buy food and ask them to compare prices and calculate portions and costs, especially on those ingredients they themselves will use in preparing a recipe.

Resources

www.cookingwithkids.com

This Website offers numerous tips, kid-friendly recipes and suggestions for safety.

www.easy-kids-recipes.com

This Website announces that it is the place for "solutions for busy people, families and kid cooking." The site provides recipes, food articles and information about subscribing to a free monthly *Easy Kids Recipes Newsletter*.

2

Traditional
Outdoor Games

Many of the outdoor games you or your parents played as children are unknown to kids today. Tag, red light/green light, hide-and-seek, Red Rover, marbles and similar games were the mainstays of outdoor, spontaneous play in years past. The games were simple, there were no age restrictions and the kids could set up the playing field and rules.

Some of these games have been reincarnated today as computer games. Your children may recognize them as electronic games with different names. But if your goal is to pry your kids away from sedentary games in front of a computer or TV screen, you can start by helping them and their friends get up a game outdoors in the fresh air.

One of the most basic outdoor running games is tag. You can start by explaining the basic rules of simple tag.

Tag

Assign one person to be the tagger or it. When that person shouts go, everyone else in the group runs away while it tries to touch someone else. If it succeeds in tagging someone else, that person become it and chases everyone else. The game can continue until everyone is exhausted or ready to play something more complicated.

Before everyone wanders inside to play computer games, ask the children if they can design a more intricate or challenging game of tag. You might be surprised at their inventiveness. If no one can come up with a workable idea, you can suggest several variations on the basic game. The following are some tag games that can add some variety to their play.

Contortion Tag

This is played by the same rules as simple tag, but the player who has been tagged must place his or her right hand on the spot where tagged–shoulder, arm, chest, leg, ankle or back. Holding that position, he or she must then run after the other players until he tags a new person to become it.

Snake Tag

Snake Tag starts by having three or four people hold onto the waist of the person in front of them to form a snake. The first person is the head of the snake and the last person is the tail. One person remains outside the snake to be it. To begin, the person who is it must catch the tail of the snake and attach on to it. The head of the snake now detaches and becomes it. The people forming the snake twist and writhe like a snake to avoid losing the head.

Heads or Tails Tag

Divide the players into two teams: heads and tails. In the center of the playing area, lay out two parallel lines about three-feet apart using chalk on blacktop, garden hoses or ropes on grass. Then lay out two boundary lines about 20 feet from the center lines for each team to cross into their safe zones. To begin, toss a coin and call out the side it lands on. If it is heads, the heads team runs toward its safe zone with the tails team in hot pursuit trying to tag them before they reach their safe zone. After each toss and run, players who were not tagged out return to their center line and play again. The game is over when one team captures everyone on the opposite side.

Red Light/Green Light

One person plays the stoplight and the others try to tag him. The children line up about 15 to 20 feet away from the stoplight who turns his back to the other children. When the stoplight calls out green light, the children move forward toward the stoplight. At any point the stoplight can yell out red light and turn to face the line of approaching children. Any children who are caught moving are out. The game continues when the stoplight turns around again and calls green light. The stoplight wins if all the children are out before anyone touches the stoplight. Otherwise, the first player to touch the stoplight wins and is allowed to be the stoplight for the next game.

An alternate way to play is to have the kids form a line on one side of a large field or yard with the stoplight in the middle. When the stoplight calls green light, the kids run toward the other side of the playing area. When the stoplight says red light, everyone stops running and whoever does not stop within 2 seconds is out. The game is over when all of the kids are out or have run across the field and back to the starting point. The last person to reach the starting point is the stoplight for the next game.

Hide-and-Seek

Hide-and-seek is a form of tag that requires the tagger or it to close his eyes and count to a predetermined number–usually between 10 and 20–at the home base while all the other players run to hide. When it calls out ready or not, here I come and rushes to find everyone, the other players try to run to base without getting tagged by it. Whoever is tagged is then it.

Flashlight Tag

Played at night, this game is a combination of tag and hide-and-seek. The tagger or it counts at the base while everyone else hides. Then taking a flashlight, it searches for the hiders, who are allowed to change hiding spots while it searches. The flashlight must remain turned on and cannot be covered. When it spots someone, he uses the flashlight to get a close enough look to identify the hider and call out his name. At this point, it can pass the flashlight to the caught person who becomes it. Or each caught player can wait until everyone has been caught, at which point the first person caught becomes it. Players can have a lot of fun outwitting the person who is it in this game. For example, they can switch hiding places by moving to a place it has already searched, or they can follow it as he searches. Some kids even like to wear dark clothes as camouflage.

Red Rover

Divide the players into two groups and line them up, instructing them to hold hands tightly. Have the two groups face each other about 20 to 25 feet apart. Select a caller from each team. The caller from one side shouts Red Rover, Red Rover, send [name of child] over. The named child then runs to the opposite side and tries to break through the line. If he is successful, a child from the opposite side must join his team. If the child fails, he must join the caller's side. The teams take turns calling until one team has all of the children or until the children run out of time. In that case the team with the most members is the winner.

Uncle Sam

A variation of Red Rover, Uncle Sam, is played by two teams lined up as if they were playing Red Rover. One team chants, Uncle Sam, Uncle Sam, may we cross your waterland? The tagger or it stands in the middle between the teams and replies, not unless you have the color [name of color]. Any member of the opposite team wearing the called color crosses to the opposite team. Those without the color run across while trying to avoid being tagged by it. Those who are tagged join it and help tag others on subsequent runs.

Marbles

The game of marbles is played within a ring 10 feet in diameter drawn on a relatively smooth dirt playing area. To begin the play, each player stands at the outer edge of the circle and rolls a marble toward a line drawn along the opposite side of the circle. The player whose marble is the closest to the outer line begins the game.

The players first position 13 marbles in an X shape at the center of the ring. Player #1 kneels at the outer edge of the ring and places one knuckle, usually the index finger, on the ground. He then places the shooter marble in the crook of the index finger and flicks it out with the thumb. If the shooter knocks another marble out of the ring while the shooter itself remains within the ring, the player confiscates the marble and takes another turn. After the first shot, the player can kneel within the ring at the point where his shooter stopped.

If, on his second play, player #1 hits a marble but neither knocks it nor rolls his shooter out of the ring, he must leave the marble and shooter within the ring while player #2 takes a turn. Player #2 then shoots from the edge and can try to knock either a marble or the other player's shooter out of the ring. If he knocks neither a marble nor his opponent's shooter out, play returns to player #1. This time he can kneel inside the ring next to his shooter. The goal is to get the shooter as close as possible to the center of the ring for subsequent shots. This type of back-and-forth play continues until all of the marbles have been confiscated.

Balloon Stomp

Finally, a let-off-steam running game–balloon stomp. Each child blows up a balloon and ties it to his ankle with string. At a signal, everyone runs around trying to stomp on or break each others' balloons. The winner is the last person with an intact balloon.

Resources

Readers Digest Great Big Book of Children's Games, (Readers Digest, 1999).

A compendium of children's games.

Safe at Play: Outdoor Safety (What Would You Do? Game Book), (Candy Cane Press, 2005).

This reference book emphasizes safety and accident prevention.

www.funattic.com

This Website features sports and outdoor games.

Rainy days provide a good opportunity to exercise your creativity. Bad weather is not an excuse to spend the day in front of the computer or the TV.

Imaginary Adventure

Offer the kids a snack if they can navigate their way through an imaginary land you create from your furniture. Older children can help you construct the imaginary land and younger kids can think up names of places in this land.

Place a blanket or sheet over the dining room table and create a cozy cave. Using chairs, tables and other furniture, drape sheets to build an obstacle course that leads to the cave. Depending on how much space and furniture you have, you and the kids can build tunnels, smaller caves and forts along the route. The kids may want to tape directional signs to the sheets with arrows pointing the way through the course or steering everyone toward a dead end. Turn off the lights, equip each child with a flashlight and urge them on their way. Meanwhile, at the end of the course, you can supply pillows, a CD player and favorite CDs in the cave and set out the promised snack.

This imaginary journey can be as simple or as complicated as you want. Your kids will probably get into the spirit of the activity and think of additions to the course. After you have set up the obstacle course, furnish extra blankets and sheets and let the kids use their own imaginations.

Hot Potato

Reminiscent of musical chairs, this classic game uses a real potato or a small ball. The players stand in a circle and you or an older child starts the music playing on a boom box or CD player. Players pass the potato around the circle until the music stops. The player holding the potato when the music stops is out. The game continues until one person is left standing in the circle. He or she is declared the winner.

Freeze Dance

A variation of hot potato, freeze dance is played by having the kids dance to fast music controlled by you or an older child. When you stop the music, everyone freezes in place. Anyone who moves is out. The winner is the last person on the dance floor.

Clapping Game

This game is a chanting game accompanied by clapping. You can either teach the kids a familiar chant or make one up yourselves. One of the better known chants is the following:

A sailor went to sea, sea, sea
To see what he could see, see, see
But all he could see, see, see
Was the bottom of the sea, sea, sea.

The clapping sequence for this chant is

A sailor went to clap-clap-clap
To see what he could clap-clap-clap
But all he could clap-clap-clap
Was the bottom of the clap-clap-clap.

A sailor went to slap knee-slap knee-slap knee
To see what he could knee-knee-knee
But all he could knee-knee-knee
Was the bottom of the blue knee-knee-knee.

A sailor went to clap-knee-high five partner
To see what he could clap-knee-high five
But all he could clap-knee-high five
Was the bottom of the clap-knee-high five.

Grasshopper or Bunny Rabbit

If you have enough space indoors, place a blanket on the floor with a beach ball (grasshopper or bunny rabbit) in the center. Ask the kids to gather around the blanket and pick it up. Have the kids pull and snap the blanket to make the grasshopper hop without touching the floor.

Table Croquet

Table croquet is a good indoor activity because it involves both a craft activity (requiring some practice in measuring) and a game activity.

To construct an indoor playing field:

1. Cut a 7 ½- by 11-inch Styrofoam™ rectangle board. Measure and cut a piece of felt to cover the board and glue it in place.
2. Cut a wooden coffee stirrer or ice cream stick in half and draw stripes at the ends. These are the stakes.
3. Using scissors, cut a small slit in the felt on either side of the playing field and insert a stake through each slit into the Styrofoam board as wickets.
4. Cut extra-long pipe cleaners into nine three-inch pieces and bend them into half hoops. Insert them through tiny slits into the playing field board as follows: two in front of each stake, one in the center of the board and two on each side in the outer areas of the board halfway between the center and stake hoops.
5. Cut two one-inch pieces from a drinking straw. Cut slits into the ends and insert a plastic coffee stirrer in each one for mallets.
6. Use marbles or beads as balls.

To play, give a mallet and ball to each player, all of whom begin the game at one stake. The players take turns hitting their balls through each wicket in the order all the participants have decided upon. Each time a player hits a ball through a wicket, he or she gets another turn. The first player to reach the opposite stake is the winner.

Bingo

Most kids enjoy playing bingo. It satisfies their competitive urges and it helps build confidence in younger children who are learning to read double-digit numbers. You can buy a game at either a toy store or a discount shop or you can make your own:

1. Take a piece of cardboard or poster board for each player and rule it off into squares.
2. Across the top horizontal line, write in letters and then fill in the rest of the squares with numbers. Be sure that each card is different from the others.
3. On a separate piece of cardboard, write the numbers appearing on the individual player cards and then cut this card into small squares, each with its own number. The caller will draw and call these numbers during the game.
4. Give the players buttons or coins to cover the called numbers on the player cards.

You may want to start and play the first game so that everyone is clear on what to do. After that, an older child can call the numbers while younger ones play their own cards. The first player to fill a horizontal, vertical or diagonal row with buttons or coins yells BINGO! and is the winner.

Funny People

Another quiet exercise involves having the children create humorous figures using index cards. Have the kids line up three index cards vertically in a column with the edges touching. On the top card ask the kids to draw a head; on the middle card, a matching body; and on the bottom card matching legs and feet. Encourage them to draw as many sets of people and animals as they want. When they have completed their sets of drawings, shuffle each set of cards and have the kids create new figures using one card from each of the three sets. Most kids enjoy creating silly creatures by combining segments of various people and animals.

Play Dough

Play dough is a kid favorite. But you do not have to buy the commercial brand; instead, you can save money by making your own. An additional bonus is that you can have the kids help you make the play dough—yet another lesson in measuring.

Here is a recipe you can try:

7 to 8 cups all-purpose flour
3 cups salt
3 tablespoons cream of tartar
¼ cup vegetable oil
4 cups hot water
food coloring (optional)

Steps:

1. Mix together all the dry ingredients.
2. Add in the oil and water and mix by hand for 8 to 10 minutes. (You can also use a mixer with a dough hook for 5 to 6 minutes.)
3. Add the food coloring to the oil and water if you want some color.
4. Store in a sealed container; and if it becomes too dry, knead in a few drops of water.

Resources

www.gameskidsplay.net

This Website contains information about children's games categorized by type of game. The site is continually updated so the information is fresh and different each time you visit.

Highlights for Children

This monthly magazine is full of ideas for children's activities, play, learning and fun. It appeals to children from ages 2 or 3 to first or second grade.

Games &
Counting

Many counting games are aimed at younger children who are learning numbers and ways to calculate. There are simple yet fun games that teach number recognition and counting.

Older children, however, often enjoy participating in simple number games and can be wonderful teachers for the younger kids. Helping younger kids can provide a satisfying sense of accomplishment and responsibility for older participants and foster cooperation among all the children.

Some of the counting games included here require no more than your enthusiasm and time. Others need some simple craft supplies. And still others are available online, ready to be downloaded and used. Just because you are discouraging your children from spending hours in front of the computer does not mean that you cannot take advantage of its resources for games. This might be an opportunity to explain to your kids that the computer can be a useful resource without becoming addictive.

Rhyming Counting Games

Once younger kids have learned how to count to 10, you can play rhyming counting games with them. Remember this one?

> One, two, buckle [Velcro™] my shoe,
> Three, four, shut the door.
> Five, six, pick up sticks,
> Seven, eight, lay them straight.
> Nine, ten, a big fat hen.

A more active game is One Potato, Two Potato:

> One potato, two potato,
> Three potato, four.
> Five potato, six potato,
> Seven potato, more.

Have the kids stand in a circle and hold out their fists with thumbs up. Make a fist of one of your hands and begin counting off each child's fists by tapping them. When you get to your own fist, tap your chin with it. Whenever you say more, have the child put that fist behind his or her back. Repeat the rhyme until one fist is left. That child is the winner and becomes the new counter.

Skip Counting

This game helps children learn to count by twos, threes, fours and so on. Use butcher paper or a large pad of newsprint and draw a grid of sequentially numbered squares. The grid can be as large or as small as you want. Write a numeral in each square. Begin by counting the individual squares in the grid in sequential order, emphasizing the numbers to be skip counted by calling them out loudly. Simultaneously, softly call out or whisper the other numbers. For example, in counting by twos, call out two, four, six and so on while whispering one, three and five. You can also have the children clap or stamp their feet when calling out the skip numbers. As the kids get into the rhythm, increase the speed of counting until you are counting entirely in the skip sequence. You and the kids will be shouting the skip numbers and barely whispering the other numbers. Eventually, everyone is counting in twos.

After the kids learn to count by twos, move on to threes, for example, three, six, nine and twelve. Older kids will join in at this point and the game may become competitive among the children.

Number Hide-and-Seek

Young children who enjoy playing hide-and-seek will like this counting game. In addition to being fun, this game teaches children to place numbers in sequential order.

Prepare a set of cards (such as index cards) each of which includes a numeral, the word for the number and a series of Xs that match the number. Ask all the kids to cover their eyes and count to 20 in unison. While they are counting, hide the cards within the room or around the yard. At your signal, the kids uncover their eyes and search for the cards. When they find all the cards, together they place them in sequential order. Younger ones can count the Xs and older readers can read the numerals and words.

Mancala

You may have heard of a counting game called mancala, but actually mancala is a term that refers to a series of games that originated in Africa and parts of the

Middle East. The basic game involves a strategy sequence of picking up all of the seeds from a hole and then sowing the seeds in such a way as to capture the most seeds.

To adapt this game into a counting game for your kids, make a board from an egg carton by removing the lid and taping an extra cup (cut from another egg carton) to each end. The extra cups are designated as banks to hold the players' winnings. Gather together buttons or stones to place in the carton. The object of the game is to win the most buttons.

Start by placing four buttons into each cup except the two extras on the ends. Player #1 begins by taking the buttons from any cup. Moving counterclockwise, he or she drops one button into each succeeding cup. Removing the buttons from the last cup into which she has dropped a button, the player continues emptying and depositing buttons as before until the last button falls into an empty cup.

Again moving counterclockwise, player #2 removes all the buttons from any cup she chooses and redistributes the buttons in the same way as the first player did. If her last button falls into a cup with three buttons, player #2 wins all the buttons in the cup. However, if a button other than the last one lands in a cup of three buttons, player #1 wins the buttons from that cup. The two players take turns until four or fewer buttons remain in the carton. The winner is the child with the most buttons in his or her bank.

Dice Counting Game

This game can be used for all levels of ability and experience. Have the kids take turns rolling three dice. The first player rolls all three dice, one after the other. The die with the highest number is set aside while the player rolls the other two dice again. The die with the higher number on the second roll is also set aside. After the player rolls the last die, she calculates the score by adding the numbers on the three dice. The highest score wins.

Older kids who are more advanced can practice multiplication skills by playing this game. Rather than adding the numbers on the dice, they can multiply the sum of the first two dice by the number on the third die.

Shell Counting Game

In a game version of the old shell game, two or more kids can get a sense of probability by guessing where an object is.

Line up four cups such as paper cups, coffee mugs or halves of plastic toy eggs. Ask all of the kids to cover their eyes and place a marble, bean, bead or coin under one of the cups. Each player tries to guess which cup is hiding the marble. Locating the marble on the first try scores 20 points, second try scores 10 points, third try scores five points and forth try scores zero. The fewer the number of guesses to find the marble, the higher the score. The first person to reach 50 or more points is the winner.

Teaching young children number recognition and sequence is an important task because it is the first step toward teaching children their phone number and address. When your children are familiar with numbers, you can help them learn their phone number and address by posting both on the refrigerator door or on a bulletin board or chalkboard in their room or in the family room. Refer to them often and help your child repeat them. Most children are quite proud of themselves when they can repeat their phone number and address by heart.

Resources

www.montessorimom.com

This Website contains a wealth of games and exercises, especially for younger children. Although many of the activities require specific tools and supplies designed for Montessori activities, the site does list sources for ordering equipment and supplies.

www.mathdynamics.com

This Website includes games and recommendations for improving math skills. The information is detailed and features instructions for using their activities and developing your own variations.

www.apples4theteacher.com

This is one of the Websites you should visit in order to download charts, worksheets and games. In addition, there are detailed suggestions about using the material at home.

www.preschoolrainbow.org

This Website features early childhood education ideas and activities that develop counting, observation and listening skills.

5

Games About Money

Teaching your kids about money is probably one of the most important responsibilities you have. And the kids are never too young to begin the lessons.

Making Piggy Banks

Papier-Mâché Piggy Bank

You and your kids can make this piggy bank out of papier-mâché:

1. Blow up a balloon to about four to six inches in diameter. Knot it and cover with papier-mâché.
2. To make the papier-mâché, tear 8 to 10 newspaper pages into one- by six-inch strips. Then make a solution of water and white glue. Briefly soak the strips in the solution and lay them carefully, one by one on the balloon, three or four layers deep.
3. For the pig's head, make a small ball of scrunched up newspaper and cover it with papier-mâché strips. Add small triangles made out of newspaper for ears; attach them to the head with strips of papier-mâché. Then attach the head to the pig's body with additional strips.
4. For the legs, make short columns of balled up paper, then cover with papier-mâché strips. You could also cut off sections of paper towel or toilet paper tubes, then cover and attach to the body with papier-mâché.
5. For the tail, make a hole in the pig's bottom and insert a rolled up piece of paper or a curled pipe cleaner.
6. After the pig dries–about two days–pop the balloon inside its body by inserting a pin.
7. Gently sand the sculpture smooth, paint with poster paints and decorate.
8. Finally, cut a hole or slit in the pig's back for inserting coins.

Games with Coins

Penny Pitch

Put a wastepaper basket or another type of container a few feet away from a line of children. One by one, have the kids toss their pennies in. After everybody has had a turn, ask those who got their pennies into the basket to line up again and move the container farther away. Repeat this until there is only one child who can get the coin or coins into the basket. He or she is the winner. The prize is the pennies.

Coin Basketball

Have the kids sit down at a table and give each one a large coin—a quarter or half dollar. Place a cup about two or three feet in front of them. Show the kids how to hold the coin upright on its rim with one finger, then flick it gently to spin it and let go. Another way to make a basket is by using your thumbs. With thumbs only, grab the coin. Then place your hands flat on the table, with the coin between your thumbs. Lift the coin up and throw it into the basket with your thumbs. Two points if you make it. Have the kids compete and the winner with the most points keeps the coin.

Cat and Mouse Game

Place two coins of the same size, (quarters, nickels or whatever you have) on a flat surface and put a third coin of any size in front of them, making sure they all touch. The third coin is the cat. Place a fourth coin, the mouse, about a foot away. (You could even add a tail to this coin with a piece of dental floss and tape.)

Make your hand into a fist with the index and middle finger pointing out. Then tap down quickly on the first two coins with these fingers. The kinetic force, or the energy of the tapping fingers, will propel the cat toward the mouse. See who can get the cat to the mouse with the fewest taps.

Coin Riddle

Question: What two coins equal 55 cents?

Answer: A half dollar and a nickel.

Crafts with Coins

Craft activities with coins are not only fun, but they also increase a child's familiarity with various coins.

Penny Note Cards

Make your own notepaper with a coin rubbing design. It makes a nice gift for grandparents or other relatives. Here are instructions to show your child:

1. Place a sheet of 8 ½- x 11-inch tracing paper over a sheet of heavy white paper. Hold them together with four paper clips, one near each corner.

2. Place the clipped papers in front of you vertically. With a ruler and a pencil, draw a very fine line dividing the papers in half horizontally. Cut them in half along this line.

3. You should now have two 5 ½- x 8 ½-inch sets of tracing and heavy paper. Fold each set in half (with the tracing paper on the outside) to make 2 ¾- x 4 ¼-inch notecards.

4. Place a coin between the tracing paper and heavy white paper, then rub it with a brown or copper-colored crayon or colored pencil to make a coin rubbing design around the words.

5. Staple the two papers together in the crease formed when you folded them in half, or glue the two papers together with a very thin line of glue around the edges of the heavy paper.

These cards can be used without envelopes, but you can also use leftover envelopes from old notecard collections or purchase notecard envelopes from a party store or card shop.

Coin Riddle

Question: When does 2 plus 1 equal 4?

Answer: 2 nickels and 1 dime equal 4 nickels.

Money Mobile

Have your kids make a mobile out of a wire coat hanger and coins made of clay:

1. Mix 1 cup of flour, ½ cup salt and ½ cup warm water.
2. Pour into five jar lids of any size (the clay does not need to thicken).
3. Draw your coin design into the clay with a pencil or another instrument. Do not forget your date, motto and initials.
4. Make a hook out of a paper clip and press it into the plaster or just make a hole big enough to pass string through.
5. Take the coins out of the lids and attach to the hanger with string or thread of different lengths.
6. Allow the clay to dry overnight.

Counting Money

Provide each child with a set of his or her own play money. You can download and print play money from the Internet (see Resources at the end of this chapter). Call out an amount of money and have the kids count out their play money to match that amount. Young children can start with pennies and older children can use play paper currency.

You can also ask the children to count out a certain amount using only specific coins or bills. Or you can have the kids practice making change. This type of activity can be incorporated into the pretend activity of playing store.

Teaching the Value of Money

Let your older children take control of a weekly grocery trip. Have them clip coupons, read ads and flyers and establish a budget for the week's groceries.

At the store, teach them how to read labels to figure the cost per serving as well as the nutritional value. Use actual money to show them how much an item costs and let them count out the money and pay for the groceries at the checkout. They will probably be surprised at how much money it costs to feed a family. They will also begin to understand why you occasionally say no to a purchase.

Saving Money

Any time is the right time to help your children open a savings account. They can deposit their allowance, the money they have earned or whatever money they have accumulated. If they add to their accounts every time they get a little extra cash, they will see their savings grow. Their money will also earn interest.

You can explain to the children that interest is the money the bank pays them for keeping their money in their savings account. For example, if typical interest payments for a savings account start at about 1 percent, the child would earn about $1 a year for every $100 he or she keeps in the bank.

Resources

http://pbskids.org/cyberchase/allgames.html

This Website offers online money games featuring the characters from the popular PBS television show *Cyberchase*.

http://canonprintplanet.com/kids_fun_money.shtml

Visit this Website to print facsimiles of U.S. money to use in money games.

www.learntosave.com/puzzles.htm

From this Website you can download puzzles about saving money.

www.moneyinstructor.com/kids.asp

Visit this Website to download exercise worksheets and play money.

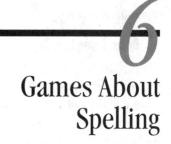

Games About Spelling

Helping your children improve–or at least review–their spelling skills is one of the easier summer activities you can do. Although there are specific spelling games you can play with your kids, using words, taking apart words and playing with words can be an ongoing part of every day's activities.

Plan, for example, to inaugurate a word of the day or week with your kids. Choose a new word at the beginning of the day or week and ask your kids to look it up in the dictionary. Discuss its spelling, meaning, antonyms and synonyms and, if your children are older, its derivation. A plus is the opportunity to discuss how to find and use the information in a dictionary. You will want to own a dictionary that is appropriate for the ages and abilities of your kids (see the Resources section at the end of this chapter). Encourage older children to use a regular dictionary, but be certain that it is not too complex or detailed for them to understand.

After they have looked up the new word, ask your kids to use it in a sentence. This will help reinforce the meaning and the context of the word or phrase. Then challenge them to use the word as often as they can during the day or week. If possible, devise a way to keep tally of how often the new word is used and award a prize to the child who uses the word most often during the day or week.

This is a good way to teach new words, but this game can also be used to review words your child has found difficult in the past. Check old spelling tests from school to find words that your child missed.

Additional Spelling Games

Some of the following games are more formalized in that you specifically set aside time to teach and play the games with your kids, while other games can be played as you go about your daily routine.

Board Game Spelling

Play any board game that requires rolling the dice. Using a set of cards on which you have written spelling words (preferably those frequently misspelled by your kids), call out a word each time it is a child's turn to roll the dice. The child must spell the word correctly in order to move forward the number of spaces as there are letters in the word. Incorrectly spelling the word means missing a turn. The child should also spell the missed word out loud at least twice and the card with the misspelled word goes to the bottom of the pile to be used again later. You yourself play the game in the usual way, simply rolling dice and moving forward as many spaces as the dice indicate.

Spelling Bingo

Give each child a blank sheet of paper and instruct him or her to create a 20-square grid by drawing of four lines across the page and five lines up and down the page. Distribute coins or beans as markers. You then call out 20 words that the children write in any square they choose on the grid.

You can then either call out and spell the words randomly, or you can give a definition of each word. The kids cover the words on their grids with the markers. The first child to cover a horizontal, vertical or diagonal row calls out BINGO! and then spells the words in his or her row.

Finding Words

Select a word and write it at the top of a sheet of paper for each child. Ask the kids to find as many words as they can using only the letters in the original word. You can make this a competition by awarding a prize or treat to the player who writes the most correctly spelled words.

A more spontaneous version of the game can be played at the breakfast table. Assign each child a brand of cereal and ask them to call out words using letters in the cereal's name while they eat breakfast. If you have time for a more leisurely game and if you allow your kids to eat presweetened cereals, give each child a cup of cereal with letter shapes and ask them to make as many words as they can from the cereal bits in the cup. Afterward, they can eat their words.

Rearranging Words

Begin with a list of words and ask the kids to add or subtract letters to form new words. For example, by changing just a couple of letters, players can begin a series of changes from the word boot to bout, boat, coat, coal, cool and so on.

Or make a word chain by adding a word with the same spelling pattern or same sound, for example, snow, slow, glow, mow, crow or day, may, sleigh, they.

Fill-in-the-blank games are fun. Give the kids a list of words, each of which has the first and last letter. Ask the kids to fill in the blanks. For example, f_ _t can become foot, fort, flat, flit.

Have kids take apart compound words and then make new words based on one of the compounds. For example, change everyone to everywhere to everything to everyday to everybody.

While you are working with compound words, ask the kids to take the last word in a compound word and make it the first word in a new compound word, for example, lighthouse to housework to workplace.

Alphabetizing is another essential skill you can work on while you are playing spelling games. Although alphabetizing seems self-evident, many kids are unsure about alphabetizing beyond the first letter in a word. One way to teach this skill is to have a child arrange her own collections, for example, of baseball cards or of book shelves in alphabetical order. You may need to help at first, and you may have to point out the advantages of maintaining books or other collections in alphabetical order. If the child needs more practice or becomes enthusiastic about doing this, turn her loose on your spice rack or CD collection.

Scavenger Hunt

Once your kids have some experience pulling apart and rearranging words, devise a scavenger hunt by asking your kids to read a passage from a book or magazine article and then find compound words, words that sound like a certain sound, words that rhyme with a sound or words that can become new if one letter is added.

Racetrack Spelling

On a large piece of poster board or newsprint, draw an automobile racetrack. Your kids can help with this. You will also need one die and some small toy cars. After rolling the die to see who starts the game, the first player is given a spelling word. If the player spells the word correctly, she can roll the die and move the toy car as many spaces as the die indicates. If the player misspells the word, he or she loses a turn and the car remains where it is.

Spelling Bees

Kids enjoy spelling bees if they are undertaken in a spirit of fun and mutual learning. You can set up an old-fashioned spelling bee in which two teams compete against each other or each individual competes against the other kids.

The kids or teams line up facing each other and you call out increasingly more difficult words. The last person standing is the winner.

Another way to set up a spelling bee is to have the moderator (you or an older child) write all the words on cards and place them in a box or hat. One at a time you display a card for a brief moment and then place it back into the container. The contestants must then write the correct spelling from memory.

Personal Dictionary

At the beginning of the summer, give each child a loose-leaf notebook filled with paper. Have the child write a letter of the alphabet at the top of each page. The first page would be A, the second page would be B and so on. Every time a child asks how to spell a word, tell her to write it correctly on the page corresponding to its first letter and add a short definition next to the word. The kids can also add in any words they seem to misspell regularly.

Each subsequent time a child asks how to spell a word, refer her to the personal dictionary. If the word is not yet there, have the child add it to the appropriate page. Because you are using a loose-leaf notebook, you can have the children add new pages for each letter as they fill up the original page.

By the end of summer the children will all have personal dictionaries that may be more helpful than the standard reference dictionary. After all, they have personally written in each word, which helps them remember the spelling, and they have looked up a definition for each word. They can tuck their dictionaries into their backpacks as a reference guide, but often they will not need to use them because they have learned many of the entries by heart.

Resources

www.scholastic.com

This Website suggests dictionaries and other reference books aimed at children of different ages. In addition, the site suggests activities and resources for kids, parents and teachers.

25 Super-Fun Spelling Games (Grades 2-4), (Scholastic, 1999).

Card games, spelling lists and other game activities for children 7 to 10 years old.

7

Games that
Improve Imagination

Helping your kids develop their imaginations can never start too soon. Even very young babies respond to stimulation that helps promote imaginative play. Just remember that at the beginning, babies consider you or older children in the family as toys. Activities that are both stimulating and fun for a baby include talking, smiling, laughing and carrying the baby.

Activities for Babies

As babies become more active, you can begin to introduce additional toys. If you want to engage a baby's attention for increasingly longer periods of time, be sure the toys you provide are interactive; that is, they allow the baby to do something while playing with them. Rattles, either purchased or homemade, make different sounds when the baby shakes them in different ways. You can make a rattle by filling an empty drink container or a milk bottle with buttons, beans or pasta–taking care to secure the lid tightly. You can even make two or three rattles, each with a different type of material to create different sounds.

When the child passes the rattle stage, you can make a drum by stretching papier-mâché strips over a coffee can. Once the material has dried, give your baby a wooden spoon to bang the drum. If you have nerves of steel, you can also turn over a saucepan or cooking pot and let your baby pound away.

Since sounds are appealing to babies, reading aloud, especially rhyming stories, is very entertaining. Encourage your baby to pound the drum or clap hands while you read.

If you have older children, do not forget that you can give them something to do as well by having them construct the baby's toys and read aloud. What may at first seem to be a chore to the older ones can become fun, especially if you encourage them to think up interactive games for the baby. They can also read to the baby and teach the little one how to clap hands or wave in time to the rhythm.

Activities for Older Kids

Children from the toddler stage to the preteen stage enjoy making up stories and acting out fantasies. You can suggest that younger children act out feelings or specific actions and older children act out a story. First, however, you need some resources and props.

Dress-Up Box

Find a large (but storable) box and begin to collect dress-up and pretend outfits. Go through your closets and gather old clothes, hats and accessories for the dress-up box. Old aprons, shawls and towels will get a lot of use. Include some old shoes or boots, purses, tote bags and brief cases. Well-washed ice cream cartons can become all sorts of hats; old socks or stockings can become animals or puppets; newspapers can become pirate hats. Check everything for cleanliness and safety—you want to remove sharp buttons or hooks and smooth sharp edges.

Cartons and Boxes

Empty cartons and boxes of all sizes are perfect for imaginative play. If you have space to store large cartons, go to an appliance store and ask for empty refrigerator or washer/dryer cartons. These can be transformed into houses or other buildings with a little glue, poster paint and cardboard and fabric scraps.

Smaller boxes can also be turned into play objects. For example, cut a wide slit into the side of a shoebox, and presto, you have a mailbox. Younger kids especially like to push items through slots (better the cardboard box than the VCR slot) and children who can read and write can post notes or letters to each other or to imaginary friends.

Other small boxes can be glued together to form a dollhouse, a zoo building or a barn. The kids can use tempera paints, glue, fabric scraps, toothpicks and cardboard pieces to create and decorate their own unique structures. These structures can be reconfigured or added on to accommodate whatever the child has in mind.

Pretend Games

Cape Capers

Supply each player with a small blanket, towel or cloth scrap to be used as a cape. Place the cloth over each child's shoulders like a cape and demonstrate how to hold the ends of the blanket or towel with hands outstretched. Have the child play make believe as you recite this rhyme together:

Flap your wings like an eagle in the sky,
Then soar like an airplane flying high.

Float like a ghost and say Woooo!
Then drift like a cloud in a sky of blue.
Become a super hero, dash and dart about.
"I'm coming to the rescue!" is what you shout.

Acting Out Directions

Encourage your children to act out actions or directions. For example, send the kids outside with the following suggestions and ask them to select the person or group who does the best job:

- Zoom like a plane.
- Stretch like a cat.
- Leap like a frog.
- Trek through the jungle.
- Move around.
- Demonstrate moving up.
- Demonstrate moving fast.

- Fly like an eagle.
- Strut like a rooster.
- Run like a cheetah.
- Move like lightning.
- Demonstrate moving through.
- Demonstrate moving down.
- Demonstrate moving slow.

Action Story

Ask the kids to choose their favorite action storybooks and to copy the actions and expressions of the characters as you read the stories out loud. You can read the story, or, if there are more than two children playing, they can take turns reading and acting. Older children can read to younger children.

Round Robin Story

This activity fosters creativity and can become a lot of fun. Rather than read a story, have the children make up their own story–a sentence at a time. You may have to provide the first sentence, but after that each child adds a sentence as the story travels around the circle of kids. A child who provides a non sequitur may turn the story in a new direction, compelling the next child to pick up the new thread and develop it. Many times the story becomes silly, yet to keep the story growing, the children need to use their imaginations and sense of humor. This game may go on for a long time, depending on the age and interest levels of the children involved.

Imaginary Trip

Ask your kids to plan an imaginary trip. The destination can be anywhere they choose, and the time period can be the present, the past, or some future time. You may want to introduce this activity at a time when you have planned a trip to the library.

There are many activities your kids can do while planning their trip. They can plan what to pack, factoring in the climate, the location and the time of year. Also, they can plan a meal using recipes and ingredients from that locale. In addition, they can check at the library for examples of music from that region.

Suggest that after completing the research on their chosen destination the kids reenact the trip in your own backyard or home. For instance, hang an old sheet on a clothesline or a large sheet of paper on a wall and let the kids paint a backdrop of their chosen place. Maybe an African plain or a street in Italy. Then help them put together some appropriate costumes and a picnic lunch of regional food. A few storybooks about the area and/or some stuffed animals to fit the scene, and you are ready to settle in for an educational lunch.

Do not be concerned if the kids mix and match different places and different time periods. As long as they are creating a place using their imaginations, they can decide what they want to do.

Books, Magazines and Charades

Carus Publishing is another good resource. Publisher of such magazines as *Cricket, Babybug, Ladybug, Spider* and *Ranger Rick*, Carus features magazines with stories, puzzles, reports and graphics suitable for various age levels. The magazines are interactive, allowing each child to use the magazine at his or her own level.

Finally, there is nothing that requires more imagination than playing charades. Divide the kids into teams and print suggestions to be acted out on slips of paper. Have each child draw a slip from a hat or container and act out the idea within a certain time limit. You can use an egg timer or a kitchen timer. Tally the score of the two teams after every child has had a chance to play.

Resources

101 Improv Games for Children and Adults, (Hunter House Publishers, 2004). This book presents the basics of improv, including warm-up games, fairy tales and narrative stories.

More Help! For Teachers of Young Children: 99 Tips to Promote Intellectual Development and Creativity, (Corwin Press, 2005). This book contains ideas for use on a daily basis with younger children.

http://kids.nationalgeographic.com

This Website offers online games that promote creativity and thinking.

8

Games that Promote Teamwork

While your main objective during the summer and school vacations is to keep your kids occupied and active, you also want to select activities that are educational as well as fun. Teaching teamwork is an important goal, and there are many games and activities that promote cooperation and teamwork while simultaneously being fun. Try a few of the following activities with your kids and their friends.

Partner Pull-up

This game helps build muscle strength and teaches cooperation. Ask the children to pair off and sit on the floor facing each other, with one player's feet touching the other's feet. Grasping each other's hands, the children pull together so that they both stand up and then return to a sitting position. This may take some time for the kids to develop a mutual working rhythm.

Circle Walk

Ask everyone to stand in a tight circle front to back. (This works best with children that are approximately the same size.) Have everyone move in closer to make the circle very tight. At your signal, everyone sits on the lap of the person behind him or her at the same time. If the circle remains connected, ask everyone to walk together as part of the circle. You can call out directions such as right, left, forward and backward.

Hula Drop

Dividing the kids into small groups of three or four, ask each child to place the tips of two fingers of each hand under a hula hoop. Then tell the kids to lower the hoop to the floor or ground without anyone's fingertips slipping off. For older kids, forbid talking or coaching.

Hula Loop

Have the kids stand in a circle holding hands. Place a hula hoop or a long loop of soft fabric over one pair of joined hands. Each child in the circle must pass the loop over his head and torso and on to the next person without letting go of hands. If you have a large circle of kids, start two loops going around.

Human Tangle

While the kids are in a circle, ask them to grab hands with two different people across the circle. Then step back while they attempt to untangle themselves without letting go of each other's hands.

Blanket Volleyball

Start with two teams, each with a blanket stretched out like a net. Toss a ball or any other soft object into one of the blankets and instruct the teams to volley the ball from team to team, using the blankets to propel it. If the game becomes too easy, toss in additional balls.

Blindfold Ball

Pair the kids into two-person teams and place a blindfold on one member of each team. Give one blindfolded child a soft foam ball and tell him to throw the ball at any other blindfolded player. The aim of the game is to get the second blindfolded player to pick up the ball and throw it at another blindfolded player. The partners of the blindfolded children guide them by the arm and provides directions and/or warnings. If a player is hit by the ball twice, the team is out. The game continues until the last pair remains alone on the field. When you have finished one round, switch the blindfolds to the other members of the pairs.

Before beginning the game, be sure to explain to all the kids how to lead someone by the arm and how to avoid collisions when blindfolded. Blindfolded players should move forward with their hands in front to prevent running into objects or obstructions. Partners should also learn to concentrate on each other's voices, so they can distinguish their own voices from those of other pairs.

Blindfold Walk

A variation of blindfold ball is blindfold walk. Pair the kids into teams and instruct the person who is not blindfolded to take his partner on a walk. Choose an area that is challenging, such as one that requires climbing over furniture, crawling under tables or walking up or down stairs. Try to stress that the guide use only verbal instructions to steer his partner on the walk. After a predetermined walk is finished, allow the kids to exchange blindfolds and play again.

Group Hide-and-Seek

This variation of the typical hide-and-seek game fosters group cooperation and teamwork. This can be played outdoors at night or inside with all of the lights off.

In this game the person chosen to be it hides while everyone else counts to 100. When the players have finished counting, they go off on their own to seek it, but when each player finds it, he hides with it until the last person finds the hiding group. Naturally, this common hiding place requires strict silence on the part of the hiders until everyone has joined the group. The last person to find the hiding group becomes it.

Goody Grab

This game is designed to teach the children that the more they work together to solve a problem and to reach a mutual goal, the more rewards they get.

For this game you will need a bag of individually wrapped candy or if you prefer, small bags of raisin or nuts. In addition, you will need a piece of cardboard or a carpet remnant large enough for two children to stand on. Place the cardboard or carpet piece on the floor, taping it down if it slides around. Scatter the candy around the cardboard on the floor far enough away from the cardboard that the candy pieces would be difficult to reach for anyone standing on the cardboard by themselves. Be sure to allow for differences in height among the contenders.

Divide the group into pairs and dare each team to get as much candy as they can by working together as a team. However each team must obey the following rules:

- Both players must stand on the board at all times.
- No part of the body or clothing may ever touch the floor. If you touch the floor, you go to the end of the line.
- No one can slide the cardboard.
- The partners must pick up the candy, not drag it or pull it toward them.
- The partners may not use anything like a stick or a belt to pull the candy toward them.
- Whatever goodies the partners pick are theirs to keep.
- When you have grabbed one piece, you have 10 seconds to continue to try before you go to the end of the line.

Begin the game by stating only these rules. If the children have trouble figuring out how to work together to get the candy, hint that one could hold onto the other while he reaches for the candy.

Guess Who?

Try this game when you are looking for something that is a little quieter. This game is most successful if the children are at or near the same level of experience.

Ask each child to select the name of a famous person, book character or TV personality and write it on a sticky note. Be sure to tell the children to keep the names a secret. Each person then places the sticky note onto another person's back.

Taking turns, each player with a sticky note on his back asks the group questions to find out his identity. The questions should be phrased so as to receive a yes or no answer. For example: Am I living? Am I female? Am I a musician? Am I a cartoon character? The players keep asking questions until they make an incorrect guess about their identity. The winner is the one who can guess his identity without making any incorrect guesses.

Resources

Safe at Play: Outdoor Safety (What Would You Do? Game Book), (Candy Cane Press, 2005).

This reference book emphasizes safety and accident prevention.

http://businessmajors.about.com

Visit this Website and click on Icebreaker Games on the left side of the opening screen. You will find icebreaker games that you can adapt to use with children.

All About
Bugs

Bugs fascinate most kids. And this interest provides you with an opportunity to develop some educational activities focusing on insects in your own backyard and in the neighborhood.

You can begin by supplying each child with a magnifying glass and a small notebook to write down his or her observations. If your children are too young to write, you may need to be the scribe or–better yet–enlist an older child to accompany a younger child and take the notes. Wander through the yard or a park and look for bugs. Write down what you see, including the location and activities of individual insects. You will be able to identify common ones immediately, but you may also encounter unfamiliar bugs that you can research later.

Camouflage

As you and your kids begin learning about the world of insects/bugs but before you begin looking for them, you may want to explain insect camouflage to your kids. Camouflage comes from the French word, camouflager, which means blind or veil. Many insects camouflage or disguise themselves for protection against other insects or animals that want to eat them. Some birds, bats, frogs and other animals consider insects a main part of their diets. Therefore, many insects use camouflage colors and patterns to blend in with their environment or conversely to warn off predators. A good example of camouflage is the praying mantis whose body often resembles a leaf or branch. Some caterpillars, too, look like twigs, and moths and butterflies use their wings to blend into their surroundings or appear as dead leaves when they are resting.

If you and your kids are aware of the ways insects use camouflage, you will be able to find and identify those insects that are hiding.

Catching Bugs

To spark everyone's interest at the beginning, show your kids how to construct an insect trap. You will need a glass jar about six-inches deep, a small board and some rocks. Instruct your kids to do the following:

1. Dig a hole in the ground and bury the glass jar, making sure the open end is level with the ground around it.
2. Pack the dirt down around the opening, right up to the rim of the jar.
3. Arrange three to four rocks around the rim of the jar.
4. Lay the small board across the rocks to create a roof for the open jar. There should be approximately one-half inch between the ground and the roof.

The bugs will crawl under the roof and tumble into the open jar. The smooth glass sides of the jar will prevent their escaping the trap and the roof will protect them from rain, birds and other predators. Have the kids check the trap several times during the day. After they have finished studying and making notes about the captured bugs, tell them to release the bugs near the jar so the bugs can return to their natural habitats.

Before releasing the bugs, however, have the kids conduct an experiment. Suggest that the kids bait the glass jar with bits of fruit, leaves or different kinds of food to see what types of bugs each bait attracts. Be careful to use only one kind of bait at a time.

Catching a Praying Mantis

Praying mantids eat and grow during the summer and then mate and lay eggs in the fall. The female lays about 12 to 40 eggs in a foamy liquid that turns into a hard protective shell. If you find a mantid eggshell under a branch in the late fall, you can cut off the branch and keep it at winter temperatures in a box in an unheated shed or garage. Do not keep it indoors at warm temperatures because the eggs will hatch early in the winter when it is too cold to release the hatched nymphs outside. In the spring, bring the box inside and watch for the nymphs to hatch.

Once hatched, the nymphs will have to be separated into individual boxes; otherwise they will eat each other. In fact, after a day or two of watching them, you should release the newborns outdoors to resume their normal life span and maturation. They will become adults during the summer and then mate in the fall. There is only one generation each year and adults die of either old age or freezing as winter comes on.

Catching Fireflies

Many parents fondly remember catching fireflies on warm nights and placing them in a glass jar along with foliage and grass. Of course, half of the fun was pounding holes in the jar lid to allow air into the container.

You can share this with your kids today as long as you have a jar, a hammer and ice pick to poke holes in the lid and a ready colony of fireflies. Unfortunately, fireflies do not appear west of Kansas in the United States and no one knows why. However, in the eastern part of the United States, you can find fireflies around ponds, streams or low spots that retain moisture. If you look for fireflies in your yard or a nearby park, search areas that are dark; fireflies do not flash in areas that are bright because it is hard for potential mates to see each other in lighted areas.

Fireflies may seem elusive because they flash so briefly. However, once you see one, it is relatively easy to scoop the insect into your hand and drop it into a jar. Just remind your kids to release the fireflies at the end of the evening. They should remain in the jar for just a short time.

Catching Caterpillars and Hatching Butterflies

You can help your kids create a butterfly hatchery in which they can place the chrysalis (the case or cocoon in which a caterpillar encloses itself while it turns into a butterfly) in order to watch the butterfly hatch. To build a butterfly hatchery, instruct your kids to do the following:

1. Assemble a large cardboard box, plastic wrap or screening, scissors, tape and a twig.
2. Cut out one side of the box and stretch plastic wrap or screening over the opening to create a viewing window.
3. Cut a flap in the back or side of the box for reaching in to feed the butterfly.
4. Poke a row of air holes on each side of the box.
5. Place a large twig in the bottom of the box, leaning against the side wall.
6. Decorate the box—a good activity for younger children—being careful not to block the flap or air holes. If you paint or glue the box, allow 2 to 3 days to dry and air out the box.

When you find a chrysalis, place it in the box, leaning against the wall. You want to try to place it so that it leans in a natural position. Now you have to wait 7 to 10 days for the butterfly to emerge.

After emerging, the butterfly will hang from the twig you have placed in the box. The butterfly will hang there about 1 to 2 hours while it pumps fluid into its wings until they expand.

Now you must start feeding the butterfly daily. Have your kids mix two teaspoons of sugar with one cup of water. Then saturate a rolled-up paper towel or a sponge with the mixture and place it into the box. You can also tightly roll a paper towel into a wick and submerge it into a cup of the mixture. Be sure the wick is higher than the cup's rim so that the butterfly can feed from it. You can feed and keep the butterfly in the hatchery box for up to 2 weeks.

Releasing the butterfly is part of the lesson for the kids. Take it to a flower garden, a field or a quiet park when outside temperatures reach at least 55 degrees Fahrenheit. You can make this into a ceremony so that the kids understand that butterflies and other insects need to be in their natural habitat rather than in captivity.

Identifying Bugs

Being able to identify bugs appeals to children, especially older kids. If you encourage them to keep a journal about the bugs they catch or observe, you should also help them develop research techniques for identifying bugs. Introduce the kids to field guides and other sources of information (see Resources at the end of this chapter).

Here is a table to help your kids begin to identify common bugs they may encounter:

Insect	Habitat	Diet	Life Cycle	Characteristics
Praying Mantis	Flowering plants, vegetable gardens	Live moths, crickets, grasshoppers, flies, spiders	Hatch and grow to adulthood during summer, mate in fall	Long, long body (½ to 12 inches), triangular head, oversized front legs held in front of face; uses camouflage
Housefly	Everywhere	Nectar, plant sap, blood, insects, dead flesh, food	Life span of 7 to 10 days, possible 10 to 12 generations in one summer; can survive winter as larvae (maggots) in protected place	Has 6 legs and segmented body consisting of head, thorax and abdomen; 2 instead of 4 wings; cannot chew so sucks up food after liquefying it; can walk upside down

Firefly	Edges of streams or ponds, rotting wood, forest brush, eastern U.S.	Earthworms, snails, slugs	Life span of 2 months	Belongs to beetle family, 4 wings, body produces light
Ladybug	Forests, fields, gardens, homes	Aphids, mealybugs, mites	Eggs hatch in 3 to 7 days, larval stage is 2 to 4 weeks, pupa stage is 5 to 7 days, adult lifespan is a few months	Member of beetle family, red with black spots or black with red spots, spots fade as bug ages, 3 pairs legs, 1 pair antennae, 4 wings, plays dead when threatened
Ant	Colonies or nests in soil near a house, under concrete, in wood, in trees	Food, sugar	Life span of 45 to 60 days, 4 stages: egg, larva, pupa, adult	Shaped like figure 8, 6 legs, antennae, transparent wings if not wingless, various colors
Bee	Colonies or nests (social bees with a queen, drones and worker bees), solitary nests for single bees in hollow tree or under roof	Flower pollen and nectar (honeybees), insects and spiders (wasps)	Life span from egg, larva, pupa to adult is 21 days, queen lives 2 to 5 years, drone lives 40 to 50 days, worker lives 1 to 4 months	Large back feet, stinger, body hairs (to hold pollen)

Did You Know...

That a spider is not an insect? Unlike insects that have six legs and three body parts, spiders have eight legs and two body regions. Most also produce a silk-like substance in order to spin webs.

Resources

http://members.aol.com/YESbugs/bugclub.html

This is the Website of the Young Entomologists Society, a group for insect, spider and minibeast enthusiasts. This nonprofit society promotes entomology, arachnology (study of spiders) and invertebrate zoology education for young people. Membership includes kids, parents, teachers and naturalists.

www.extension.umn.edu/distribution/youthdevelopment/DA6892.html

This Website from the University of Minnesota Extension Service describes how to collect and preserve insects.

www.uidaho.edu/so-id/entomology/caterpillars.htm

This Website is a resource to identify individual caterpillars.
http://whatsthatbug.com/caterpillar.html

This Website also provides identifying characteristics of caterpillars.

The Very Hungry Caterpillar, (Philomel, 1981)

This book, aimed at preschool children, describes a hungry caterpillar growing up to become a beautiful butterfly. It provides an accurate discussion of the life cycle of caterpillars/butterflies while appealing to younger children.

www.monarchwatch.org

Visit this Website to order monarch butterflies to study.

Peterson Field Guides®, including A Field Guide to Beetles, and A Field Guide to Insects, (Houghton Mifflin, 1997).

http://ohioline.osu.edu/hyg-fact/2000/2060.html

This Website provides an Extension Fact Sheet HYG 2060-04 entitled "Spiders In and Around the House," which offers detailed information about spiders.

Water Games

Hot summer days seem to call out for cooling water games. There are several types of games: Some are played outdoors in the yard while others are played in a swimming pool. While a pool is ideal for water games and sports, you do not have to have a pool to keep your kids occupied with water games.

Remember, however, that whatever type of water games you and your kids play, your first priority is safety. Any kind of activity involving water–from a bucket to a bathtub to a swimming pool–requires adult supervision and awareness of each child's skill level. In addition, you should take steps to prevent water accidents:

- Stay with your kids when they are near water even if they can swim.
- Teach your kids about water safety and how to swim.
- Learn CPR–enroll in a course.
- Empty buckets, tubs and wading pools when you are finished with them.

Water Activities for Very Young Children

Toddlers and preschool-age kids may not be old enough or skilled enough to play games with buckets or hoses or to participate in pool sports. However, here are some simple activities that young kids will enjoy.

Do-It-Yourself Paddle Boat

To make this toy, you will need a scrap board six-inches long, three-inches wide and one-half-inch thick. Also gather three Popsicle™ sticks, duct tape or tacks and a rubber band.

Attach two Popsicle sticks using tape or tacks on both sides of the board two-thirds of the way toward the back. Stretch the rubber band between the two Popsicle sticks. Break or cut the third Popsicle stick in half and wind it in the rubber band as a paddle. Place in water–such as a bucket or bathtub–and watch the boat paddle across the water surface as the rubber band unwinds. Most young kids enjoy rewinding the paddle stick over and over to make the boat race through the water. Tip: Save the other half of the third Popsicle™ stick to replace the first half when it breaks or disappears in the water.

Ice Cube Melt

Line up several young kids into two teams and place an ice cube in the hands of the first player on each team. The first player rubs the cube until his or her hands become too cold and then passes the cube to player #2. Continue passing the cube until it melts. The first team to melt the cube wins.

Ice Cube Toss

Have two teams sit on both sides of a filled wading pool, facing each other. Empty a tray or two of ice cubes into the pool and instruct the kids to remove the ice cubes using only their toes or feet. Use a timer to set a time limit so that you can count the cubes before they melt. When the timer rings, the team that has removed the most ice cubes wins.

Water Activities for Older Kids

Bucket Games

These games use buckets and you may want to locate sources for old, yet serviceable buckets. Try flea markets or garage sales.

Bucket Relay Games

These games require at least two teams of kids. For the first game, line up the kids and provide each team with an empty plastic cup and a sponge. Place a bucket of water several feet in front of the teams. The second person in line on each team places the empty cup on his or her head. The first person on each team runs to the bucket of water, dips the sponge and runs back to her teammate to squeeze the sponge into the cup. When the cup is full, the second person empties it onto the first person's head; the first person then goes to the end of the line. The team continues the process through all of its members until the entire line has had a turn. The first team to finish is the winner.

Another team relay game uses a bucket of water and a plastic cup and spoon for each team. Place the cup at the finish line. Each team member in turn fills the spoon with water from the bucket and pours it into the cup. The first team to fill its cup is the winner.

Or have the teams form a single-file line at the head of which is a bucket of water. At the end of the line place a pitcher or large jar with a line drawn on it. The person at the head of the line dips a sponge in the bucket of water and passes the wet sponge over her head to the person behind who then passes the sponge through her legs to the following person. The sponge is passed over heads and through legs until it reaches the last person in front of the pitcher. That person squeezes water from the sponge into the pitcher and runs the sponge back to the front of the line. Everyone moves back one position. The play continues until the pitcher is filled up to the line. The team that fills its pitcher first is the winner.

The back-to-back relay game requires an empty bucket for each team and bucket of balloons half-filled with water. Pair off the kids in each team and assign them to one of the buckets of water balloons. Place each team's empty bucket about 15 feet away. Instruct each pair of children to place a water balloon between both of their backs, walk to their empty bucket and release the water balloon into the empty bucket. If the balloon breaks, the pair must go back and get another balloon. Set a timer and when the timer rings, the team with the most water balloons in their bucket is the winner.

Bucket Obstacle Course

Arrange an obstacle course using lawn chairs or furniture. Place two buckets filled to the brim with water at each end of the course. The first racer on each team carries a full bucket to the end of the course, trying not to spill any water. At the end of the course, the runner picks up the second bucket and returns to the starting point. Continue this series until every team member has had a turn. The team with the most water left in the two buckets is the winner.

Water Balloon Games

Volleyball

This requires two teams, two sheets or blankets and one volleyball net. Each team stands on their side of the net holding the sides of the sheet or blanket. Place five water balloons in the middle of one team's sheet. This team tosses the balloons to the other side and the opposing team tries to catch the balloons in its sheet and toss them back. Play the game by volleyball rules, replacing balloons as needed.

Target Practice

Have two teams face off within a measured-off space. The first player on each team holds a trash can lid or other deflector while an opposing team player tries to hit her with three water balloons. If the player is hit on the body, the opposing team receives a point. If the player deflects the balloons with the trash can lid, her team receives a point. Each pair takes a turn. The team with the most points is the winner.

Water Balloon Toss

Begin with pairs of players and give each pair a water balloon. Have each player toss the balloon to their partner. After each toss, both take a step backward. Continue until one pair is left with an intact water balloon.

Garden Hose Games

If you have a garden hose and lawn sprinkler, you can set up some fun games for hot days.

Sprinkler Freeze

Have the kids in their swimsuits dance around the sprinkler. Designate one player to control the on and off positions of the sprinkler from a spot that cannot be seen by the other players. When the sprinkler starts, the dancers must freeze in place–and get soaked in the process. Anyone still dancing when the sprinkler starts is out. When the sprinkler stops, the kids dance around the sprinkler again. They should take turns controlling the sprinkler. The last person is the winner.

Sprinkler Catch

Position your kids around an oscillating or impact sprinkler. When the spray of water passes by, players try to fill plastic cups without moving their feet. If a player takes a step, she must dump the water in the cup over her head. The first one to fill a cup is the winner.

Jumping the Hose

One child holds the hose and directs a stream of water close to the ground. The other players jump over the stream of water. Gradually, the player holding the hose raises the stream. If a player touches the stream while jumping over it, he or she is out. The last person is the winner.

Water Slide

You can construct your own backyard water slide that will provide hours of fun. You need a backyard with a grassy hill and about 30 feet of thick plastic sheeting, available at home stores and hardware stores (do not use plastic trash bags because they will tear and bunch up). Clear the hill of rocks and any other debris and then position the plastic making sure to secure the corners with U-shaped plastic garden stakes. Place a sprinkler so that it sprays on the sheeting. Direct the kids to take turns sliding at timed intervals. Be certain one kid is off the slide before another one starts.

Resources

http://raisingchildren.net.au/articles/safe_fun_with_water.html

Visit this Website for detailed information about water safety.

www.funattic.com/game_water.htm

This Website includes water games that can be played in a swimming pool.

11

Beading, Knitting & Embroidery

Beading, knitting and embroidery are handicrafts that not only require hand motor skills but develop them as well. You can find enough types of crafts in these activities to appeal to varying age levels of kids and adults. In addition, these activities do not have to be gender-specific. Both boys and girls can learn to bead, knit and embroider, particularly if the result is something they want to use, wear or play with.

Beading

Mention beading and everyone's first thought is jewelry. Yet there is more to beading than just making jewelry. Once you collect a wide range of supplies, you and your kids can make not only jewelry but musical toys as well as action figures. You can even make your own beads.

Beading Supplies

Many people get started beading when someone gives them a bead kit as a gift. It may be a good idea to start that way too. In that way, if your kids do not show an interest, you have not invested much in supplies.

You can collect a wide array of beads by shopping at a craft store where beads are sold in bags or by making your own beads. When you shop for beads, also look for cords or strings, pliers, wire cutters and tweezers. By shopping with coupons or during sales, you can accumulate a good supply of different beads without spending too much money.

Beading Projects

Here are some beading projects your kids can try:

Earrings for Non-Pierced Ears
    1. Cut two lengths of string or decorative cord about 10-inches long.
    2. Select four sets of beads.

3. Knot one end of the string and slide on one set of beads. Then slide on the second set of beads in reverse order and knot the other end of the string.

4. Repeat the process with a second string.

5. To wear, drape a string evenly over each ear.

Bracelet

1. Spread out some beads on a towel and ask your child to arrange them in the order he likes.

2. Cut an elastic cord six inches longer than the circumference of your child's wrist and knot one end.

3. Ask your child to string the beads in the selected order and then tie the ends of the cord together.

4. Be sure the bracelet slips over your child's hand.

5. Finish by brushing clear nail polish on the knot.

Beaded Curtain

1. Measure the height and width of the door.

2. Cut a bamboo rod (available at hardware stores or garden shops) to fit the width.

3. Cut 20 pieces of black or brown yarn to fit the length of the door, adding four extra inches to each strand.

4. Cut 300 clear drinking straws into random widths.

5. Begin each strand by sliding on an anchor bead followed by a piece of straw and another bead. Continue sliding on beads and straws until the entire strand of yarn is full. Tie a knot at the end. Repeat this process until all the yarn strands are completed.

6. Tie the yarn strands onto the bamboo rod and space out evenly. Glue each yarn strand into place.

7. Attach the rod to the door jam with cup hooks or with a curtain rod.

Knitting

Knitting is another handicraft that improves a child's dexterity. It is usually better to teach knitting to children who are old enough to count and who have developed fine motor skills. However, younger children can learn finger knitting, which requires only their own fingers and some yarn. In fact, finger knitting is the ultimate take-along activity, especially on airplane trips where knitting needles are banned. And it does not have to be simply a time-killing activity. Finger knitting produces a long thin strip of stockinette stick, the basic stitch of regular knitting. You can use these strips to make belts, ties, straps or even scarves if you use several strips.

Regular knitting is the simple creation of fabric from yarn by forming a row of initial stitches of twisted loops of yarn on a knitting needle. A second needle is then used to grab and pull a length of yarn through a loop to create a new stitch. By using different stitches and colors of yarn, you can create intricate patterns that are the basics of a garment or project.

Even though the process of knitting sounds complex, it can be a simple technique that is best learned from someone else who is proficient. If you know how to knit, then you can teach your kids the basics. If you are not a knitter, then look for relatives or friends who can teach your kids (and even teach you!). There are also many classes designed for children; check your local schools or craft supply stores for classes. Finally, surf the Internet for tutorials that teach knitting.

Knitting Supplies

Your basic supplies are yarn and knitting needles. Beginners should use medium to large needles because that will make the process go faster, and the knitter can see progress more quickly. Choose wooden needles since they are less slippery and thus less likely to drop a stitch. You also want to select needles that are not too sharp or too long. Needles made of wood or plastic are best.

Try to offer a variety of yarn to your kids to work with on their projects. For their first project, purchase enough yarn to finish the item. Beginning knitters lose interest if they cannot finish a project or if they have to use scraps or insufficient amounts of leftover yarns. This doesn't mean you need to buy expensive yarn; just try to find inexpensive yarn that comes in different colors, textures and weights so that your kids can be creative in designing projects.

Knitting for Charity

Many children's hospitals or family shelters appreciate donations of handcrafted toys and garments. Check with your church or local chamber of commerce to find a program in which your kids can participate. Or maybe you can start such a program in your neighborhood. Visit *www.artistshelpingchildren.org/ charityknittingforchildren.html* for more information.

Embroidery

Like knitting, embroidery is a craft best learned from someone skilled in the art. Also like knitting, you can look for classes and/or Internet tutorials to help you and your kids master the art of embroidery. For example, visit *www.secretsof. com/content/2000* for free embroidery tutorials.

Interest your kids in embroidery by pointing out that this skill is used not just for samplers or dainty handkerchiefs. They can embroider designs on their jeans or shirts, on scrapbook covers, on journal covers and on gifts. Visit *www.secretsof. com/embroiderytips/free_embroidery_designs.htm* for free designs. Better yet, encourage the kids to create their own designs–that is often the most fun. You can use graph paper to sketch out the design so that it is easy to follow.

Visit your local craft store for kits and instruction booklets. If you buy a kit, be sure to read the list of supplies needed so that you can gather everything at one time. Both you and your children should read the kit's instructions to be certain you understand the steps. Have your kids select a variety of colors of embroidery floss, several needles, hoops and other equipment needed to create their designs.

Very young children may not possess the ability or the interest to work on an embroidery project. However, some kits and Websites provide simple, large-stitch embroidery patterns that a young child can master with a little help. Be especially careful with sharp needles. Additionally, young children may enjoy watching you patch their jeans or play clothes with embroidery patterns. They can learn as you work.

Resources

The following books and Websites provide basic processes and individual projects for people who like to do beading, knitting and/or embroidery.

The Beaded Object: Making Gorgeous Flowers & Decorative Accents, (Sterling Publishing Co., Inc., 2002).

Beautiful Beads/How to Create Beautiful, Original Gifts and Jewelry for Every Occasion, (Chilton Book Co., 1994).

www.kidskitscrafts.com/kids_knitting.shtml

> This Website offers kits for making knitting craft objects for kids. Each kit is self-contained with instructions and all the necessary supplies.

www.kidskitscrafts.com/embroidery.shtml

> This Website offers kits for making embroidery craft objects for kids. Each kit is self-contained with instructions and all necessary supplies.

www.dltk-kids.com/type/crossstitch.htm

> This Website explains how to cross stitch, make patterns and select embroidery supplies. It also offers some easy projects for kids to make.

12

Learning to Paint

Painting is one of those activities that appeals to children of all ages. This is because there are so many painting techniques and materials that anyone, regardless of skill level, can enjoy the process. In fact, for young kids, painting is about the process and not necessarily the product. That is why a child considers his or her painting a work of art whether or not anyone else understands it or enjoys it.

Because the approaches to painting are so versatile, this is a good opportunity to teach your kids how to step out of the ordinary and into their own imaginations. You do not have to just paint with a brush on a canvas. Encourage your kids to be creative. Instead of brushes, use parts of your body–fingers, toes, feet, legs or arms. Or paint with cotton swabs, feathers, toothbrushes, a fly swatter, rope, yarn or sticks. Stamp or stencil with sponges, Styrofoam™, corks, leaves, cookie cutters or vegetables. Combine media by using crayons with paint for a different look. Try different effects such as splatters, drips or swirls. All of these techniques can be fun, and–best of all–each one is messy.

Supplies

Paint

When you look for paint, be sure that you buy paints designed for use by children, that is, nontoxic and washable. That way you do not have to worry about young kids getting paint in their mouths or all over their clothes. Most craft stores or Websites have a children's section where you can find safe paint. Crayola® brand products are safe.

Of course, you can also make your own paint and the following recipes will be handy on days when your kids want to paint and you have run out of it.

1. Crack one egg and separate the yolk from the white.

2. Place the yolk in a bowl and mix in one-half teaspoon of water and food coloring.
3. Use a separate bowl and another yolk for each color.
4. You can use this mixture to paint on heavy paper or on sugar cookies before they are baked.

Paper

Look for large pads of art paper or even brown craft paper. Save cardboard scraps from packaging. Try to have a variety of sizes, weights and colors of art paper. Remember, you can also use Styrofoam pieces or fabric. If your kids progress to painting on canvas, watch for sales on prestretched canvas frames. You can realize good savings if you buy these items when they are on sale.

Brushes

Brushes vary in both quality and price, so you want to be economical when you shop for brushes. Ordinary paintbrushes that are found in craft stores, dollar stores or drugstores are more than adequate for your budding artists. Naturally, you will teach your kids how to clean and store their brushes, but the life span of a paintbrush among children is limited. So do not spend a great deal of money on paintbrushes.

Clean-Up Supplies

Spread several layers of newspapers over the work area. If you have a thin plastic drop cloth or tarp, cover the table before you lay out the newspapers. Pass out old shirts or play clothes to the artists and line up several rolls of paper towels and a stack of clean rags. If you are working somewhere away from a sink, fill a bucket with warm, soapy water into which the kids can dip their hands if they become covered with paint–this is especially important when fingerpainting.

Getting Started

An easy way to start is to set up a work area complete with supplies and clean-up materials. Encourage each child to choose what he wants to do. If interest starts to flag, divide the kids into teams and have them collaborate on a piece. Very young kids may be receptive to learning about shapes, colors or texture. Show them how to build a painting around some of these simple concepts.

For those who want to experiment, set out the supplies for making their own paint or for adding a collage to the painting. Or talk about famous pieces of art–their styles, colors, light values. Ask the kids if they would like to take an excursion to an art museum or to a gallery to learn more about painting and painters. Listen carefully to their questions or opinions; you may be able to start art appreciation sessions based on the kids' interests.

Activities

For a fun afternoon, here are a few painting activities your kids can do in addition to painting on paper or canvas or instead of them.

Finger Painting

You can buy finger paints and special paper created to accept finger paint. You can introduce very young children to the sport of finger painting with instant pudding on cardboard or cookie sheets. Once instant pudding is mixed as directed and sets, it has the same consistency as finger paint. While it may seem wasteful to use food in this way, at least pudding is safe when toddlers lick their fingers.

Splatter Painting

Dip an old toothbrush into paint and hold it head up in front of you. Show your kids how to draw a Popsicle™ stick across the bristles, but away from you, so that paint splatters on the paper and not on the painter. This works best with an easel or the paper propped up against a fence or a protected surface. This can be very satisfactorily messy.

Toothbrush Painting

Use an old toothbrush instead of a paintbrush. If you want to slip in a dental hygiene lesson for your young kids, draw a set of teeth on some gray or tan paper and show them how to use the paint to clean and brighten the teeth. Then use the toothbrush to paint a face around the teeth.

Swirl Painting

Fill a bowl with warm water and dishwashing soap. Add some paint and froth the water until bubbles appear on the surface. Dip a sheet of paper on the surface of the bubbles; the paint film will stick to the paper and form a pattern. Let the paper dry. Ask the kids if they like the effect and how they could change the appearance of the final painting.

Another way to do this technique is to drop paint on the smooth surface of the water and use a toothpick or stick to swirl the paint around. Again, dip the sheet of paper and see what pattern adheres to the paper. These two techniques are used in the dip method of swirl painting, which resembles marbleizing.

The other common method of swirl painting is the drip procedure. Drip thinned paint in various colors onto the paper or canvas. Allow the paints to run together to create patterns. The painter can control the final result by moving the paper or canvas around to achieve an effect. Kids of all ages like to try these techniques just to see how the painting will turn out.

Sponge Painting

Dip a sponge in a tray of paint and lightly pat onto paper. You can try different colors or different sponges. Very young children might like to paint a beehive using yellow paint and coarse sponges. When the paint has dried, they can fill in bees and other hive features with markers. The hive scene could then be incorporated into a larger nature scene. Let your kids work outward from the beehive as far as they want.

Symmetrical Paintings

Fold a piece of paper in half and paint a scene or design on one half. While the paint it still wet, fold the halves together and press. Each half now has the same picture.

Wax Resistance Painting

Wax and paint do not mix, so you can show your kids how to use wax to mask out areas of the drawing that they do not want to be painted. Use a wax candle or crayons to draw on a sheet of paper. Then wash over the wax with water-based paint. The wax on the paper repels the water in the paint. This technique can be used for painting or to make greeting cards or signs.

Potato Stencil Painting

Very young children love this activity. Cut a potato in half and carve a relief design on the flat side. Dip the potato into paint and stamp the design on paper. This is a good method for making gift wrapping paper, and most kids will happily stamp out as much gift wrap as you want.

Art Show

Once your kids have finished their painting activities and their work has dried, what do you do with the works of art? This is the time for you and the children to decide how to display the work. Is there a hallway you could use as a gallery (with masking tape to prevent damage to walls)? Do you have a blank wall in a playroom or basement? A spot on the front porch?

You will need to create some type of gallery, even if you can display only one piece by each child at a time. Ask the kids to help you establish a rotating schedule so that everyone's art can be hung and enjoyed. Remember, if painting and other art activities are not accompanied by art appreciation, the kids may lose interest, so you want to work with the kids and the rest of the family to maintain a home art gallery for everyone's pleasure.

Resources

The Ultimate Kids Painting Book, (Grace Publications, 2001).

This book features basic painting techniques for kids and recommendations for safe products for parents.

Painting Techniques (Art for Kids), (Walter Foster Publishing, 2004).

This book contains step-by-step painting instructions for kids plus traceable patterns to get started.

http://gardenofpraise.com/art.htm

This Website offers art appreciation lessons for kids complete with the artists' biographies, worksheets and links.

13
Sidewalk
Art

One of the advantages of sidewalk art is that the diversity of the activities means there is something for every child to do–from the youngest to the oldest. Toddlers can scribble and mix colors, and older preschoolers can draw pictures and designs. Still older kids can mark off games such as hopscotch, or create layouts of buildings or towns. This is another opportunity for you to encourage imagination and creativity.

Supplies

Gather all the supplies together before you start. At the minimum, you will need chalk (or pastels, which are more vibrant in color but also more expensive) or liquid sidewalk paint. You can buy either one or make your own. Homemade chalk is less expensive and a perfect opportunity for your kids to practice their measuring skills.

Homemade Chalk
1. Line a cookie sheet with wax paper or foil and set aside.
2. Gather empty toilet paper tubes and cover one end of each tube with duct tape.
3. Loosely line each tube with wax paper or foil so that the chalk mixture does not stick to the paper of the tube.
4. Place tubes, sealed end down, on the cookie sheet.
5. In a separate bowl, mix together two cups of warm water, two cups of Plaster of Paris and two tablespoons of powered or wet tempera paint. The best way to do this is to pour water into the bowl and then gradually sprinkle Plaster of Paris into the water, stirring thoroughly. Be sure to stir all the lumps out before adding paint.
6. Pour the mixture into the tubes and tap the side of the tube to release any air bubbles.
7. Dry one to two days and then peel the tube off the chalk.

Warning: Plaster of Paris will harden even under water, so do not rinse the bowl or utensils down the drain. Hose out the bowl outside in an alley or gutter to save your plumbing. Or use an old bowl and utensils that you can throw away. Because of this, you may want to make chalk from eggshells.

1. Wash and dry four to five empty eggshells and grind them into powder and set this aside. The kids can grind them outside with a rock.
2. In another bowl, pour one teaspoon each of flour and very hot tap water and one tablespoon of eggshell powder (this will make one stick of chalk).
3. Mix in the eggsheel powder until the substance looks like paste.
4. Add food coloring if desired.
5. Mold the paste into a chalk stick and roll tightly into a paper towel.
6. Allow three days for the stick to dry.
7. You can triple this recipe and mold it in a toilet paper tube if you want a very large stick.

Homemade Paint

This is a simple recipe your kids can put together.

1. Mix together one-fourth cup of cornstarch, one-fourth cup of cold water and six to eight drops of food coloring.
2. Repeat for different colors.
3. If the mixture seems too dry, add a little water.
4. If you mix each color in a covered recycled plastic food container, you can keep the leftovers for another day.

This paint is safe to use, washes off easily and is economical compared to chalk. You can even do large murals or paintings on sidewalks.

Other Supplies

If you plan to use chalk and paint, you will need sponges, brushes and old rags to feather or blend the colors. Knee pads are optional (although you may want a pair), but a water source is important—the kids will need to wash off hands, knees and legs as well as to drink water periodically. You may want to tape some large garbage bags together to cover works-in-progress during meal breaks or when it rains. Plastic drop cloths work as well. And cleanup materials are important; be sure to have a hose or pail of water, paper towels and rags. Finally, do not forget sunscreen and hats for the kids.

Getting Started

First, select a suitable place to create sidewalk art. Naturally, your own sidewalk or driveway is ideal, but if you to expand beyond the home base to do a larger project, be certain you do not encroach on someone else's property without permission. Most people will not care, but some will not want to track chalk dust into their homes.

If you have several children involved in sidewalk art, avoid territorial disputes by marking off individual plots for each child to use. On the other hand, you could suggest that the kids work together as a team in planning and executing their work. This is especially helpful if someone wants to layout a town, race track or large board game. When everyone is ready to begin, lay out the art supplies, point out the cleanup materials and let the games begin.

Activities

You can start by letting everyone do what he or she wants. If you have some very young children in your group, you can give them squirt bottles filled with water and let them decorate the sidewalk. If interest wanes among all the kids, suggest the following activities:

Sidewalk Village

Have the kids lay out a village, shopping center, farm or zoo. This can be an individual or group activity. Suggest that the kids map out their ideas ahead of time on a section of sidewalk that can be washed off. As the layout becomes more complete, bring out some toy cars for the streets or animals for the farm and zoo. If there is a horse-crazy little girl in your group, suggest that she sketch out a corral and bring out her toy horses.

If you expect this activity to continue for a long time, you could alternatively lay a large piece of craft paper on the sidewalk and have the kids plan their layout on the paper, using markers. This way, the kids do not smudge or erase their chalk lines while they play. In addition, you can fold the paper and use it again at a later time.

Follow the Leader

This game requires several children. One child draws footprints of a certain animal or animals in a trail, either around the block or in wiggling and turning lines. The other children guess the identity of the animal and then follow the trail imitating it. The animals can be simple house pets such as dogs and cats or animals found at the zoo or at a farm. Ask if anyone wants to make up an imaginary animal and then teach the others how to act and walk like it.

Capture

Instruct the kids to draw a large house or building with windows, doors, chimneys, steps, porch, garage and gate (a driveway or large paved area is a good site for this). Draw a baseline about five feet away from the building (four feet if the children are younger).

Take turns tossing a Frisbee® onto the house. When the disk lands on a section that can be captured (like a window or gate or steps), mark the capture with the child's initials. After every section is captured, the winner is the one with the most initialed sections.

If a Frisbee lands on a section already captured, the thrower loses a turn. Also, a disk only halfway over a line does not count. You may end up being the referee, or you can assign one child to oversee the game.

Hangman

Suggest that the kids play tag as part of a hangman game. Use sidewalk chalk to draw the gallows and fill in the person on the gallows. Each child draws her own gallows and fills in a part each time she is tagged. The first person to fill in the gallows loses. The winner is the child who is tagged the least number of times.

Follow the Path

Assign one child the task of drawing a weaving, winding path on contiguous sidewalks. Then challenge the roller skaters in your group to skate along the path. Children without skates could try to ride their scooters or bikes along the trail. The more skilled the kids become, the more snaky or coiled the path can be. This is most likely to lead to some sort of competition.

Old Standbys

Sidewalk chalk is the medium of choice for some old standbys. Hopscotch is always a favorite or you could suggest tic-tac-toe. Artistic kids who can visualize object in their heads can create connect-the-dots pictures for the others to play. One child can be drawing the dots for a new design while another child completes an earlier one.

Resources

www.kuzsports.com/spray_chalk.htm

> This Website describes a spray chalk product that is safe to use on any surface and washes away with water.

www.acminet.org/Sidewalk_Chalk.htm

> This Website from the Art & Creative Materials Institute provides a list of sidewalk chalk products that have been certified as safe.

Having a Barbecue

One of summer's nicest traditions is the outdoor barbecue. Whether you grill and picnic in your own backyard or transport the party to a nearby park or beach, the casual atmosphere and grilled food are a standard summer treat.

As part of teaching your kids about cooking, you should include the fine art of barbecuing. You can include all ages by simply tailoring the tasks to meet each child's abilities. For example, toddlers and preschoolers can be in charge of buns and breads or plastic containers of condiments. Older kids can help with food preparation and serving. And mature preteens and teens can be taught how to start a charcoal fire or operate the gas grill. Just be certain that each child is capable of doing the job assigned to him or her.

Safety First

Children are naturally curious about whatever is going on, and that includes barbecuing food. Consequently, they can be found around the grill. Younger children are often at eye level with the top of the grill, making an accident even more likely to occur. Older kids may jostle to get a look, and some may even try to flip a burger. This is why you must establish non-negotiable safety rules about the grill and outdoor cooking before you even start the fire.

Be sure your kids understand the following rules:

- An adult must be present at all times while grilling.
- You must play running games far enough away from the grill so that no one collides with the grill. If the area is too small to play safely, find something else to do that is not in the vicinity of the grill.
- You must not stand next to the grill or touch it even when it is cooling down after the cooking is done.
- You must call an adult immediately if you see a fire, flames or burning embers on the ground. Do not try to put the fire out by yourself.

You yourself must abide by some safety rules as well:

- Keep lighting fluid and other flammable materials out of the reach of children.
- Do not use a propane grill on a balcony, terrace or roof. Do not use a charcoal grill on a balcony unless there is a 10-foot clearance around it.
- Place a fire extinguisher and/or a bucket of water or a garden hose near the grill. (However, do not extinguish a grease fire with water; instead use the fire extinguisher.) If a fire involves a propane tank, evacuate the area and call 911.
- Be sure the barbecue grill is in working order before you light it.
- Follow manufacturer's instructions for lighting the grill.
- Do not light a grill indoors or in a garage.
- Do not leave a grill unattended. If your grill is on a concrete or hard surface, draw a chalk line several feet out from the grill to designate a safety zone into which children cannot step.
- Allow ashes to cool completely before disposing of them.

Make a point of telling everyone in your household about these rules.

Planning a Barbecue

If you decide to have a family or neighborhood barbecue, enlist your kids in the planning stage. Talk about the menu and ask for ideas. Most kids are happy with hot dogs and hamburgers, but you can suggest other dishes that will be just as appealing while being less run-of-the-mill. How about pizza? Meat or vegetable kebabs? Or just grilled vegetables, starting with corn on the cob.

Ask the kids what they would like as side dishes. Baked beans are usually a hit, and you can make them ahead so that your attention is not divided between the grill and the kitchen. Teach your kids how to spice up a can of baked beans, allowing them to taste as they work.

Plan other dishes that can be made ahead. Outdoors is where the action will be, and neither you nor your kids want to be inside when the party is outside. Adults like potato salad while kids often prefer cold pasta salad. Either can be made ahead, and the kids can help by shelling hardboiled eggs or mixing the salad.

You can plan desserts that can be prepared and waiting before the party starts. Fresh fruit salad always tastes good on a hot day, or you can make juicicles or ice cream sandwiches if you have freezer space. Offer ice cream cones and set out small dishes of toppings such as sprinkles or nuts to dip the cones into. Another option is to bake a pie or brownies the day before. Ask the kids about their preferences and decide together who can cook or help cook each dish ahead of time.

Other Activities

If the barbecue is to be a celebration or an occasion, have your kids help plan the decorations, especially if the party is for one of them. This is an opportunity for an arts-and-crafts lesson. Discuss decorations and delegate the creation of banners, streamers, placemats and signs to the kids, based on age and skill levels. Talk about a theme and colors. Decide if you need to make a trip to a party store or the drugstore for party goods. Here is an opportunity for a math lesson: Ask the kids to figure out cost per item if they buy goods or make them. Maybe their friends and guests could help create the decorations when they arrive while you start the grill and put the finishing touches on the food.

Do not forget to plan some games and other activities. Let the kids take the lead in this if the party is to include children. If you own or can borrow a badminton or croquet set, you can set these up. Depending on space, you can set up a baseball or mini soccer game. And there is always sidewalk art, balloon toss, tag, hide-and-seek and Frisbee®. You can even play potato sack races (using old pillow cases for the children). Remember, when children are involved, err on the side of activities and games rather than food and decorations. This will probably be the emphasis if your children help plan the barbecue.

Barbecuing

Despite your carved-in-stone rule about no children near the grill, you may want to allow older kids to help with the cooking. Just be certain they do not wear any clothes that can dangle in the fire and that they use long grilling utensils. The kids should take turns since more than one cook at a grill can lead to jostling or accidents. Show them how to turn hamburgers and hot dogs and how to grill vegetables properly. You may also want to try something a little different. Have a child brush pizza dough with olive oil, first on one side and then the other. Grill one side over a medium flame until the dough begins to bubble. Lightly brush the top with oil again and flip to grill the other side. Then move the dough to a cool part of the grill while the child adds the toppings. Slide the dough back over low heat until the toppings are warm and/or melted.

The traditional s'more is always popular. Top a graham cracker with a square of chocolate and a marshmallow and place it on a piece of foil on the grill to melt. The foil prevents the chocolate from dripping into the coals. Or show the kids the old classic: toasted marshmallows. Slide a few marshmallows onto skewers and hold them over the coals until browned and melted.

If you and the kids decide to serve marshmallows—or meat or vegetable kebabs—instruct the kids how to make skewers ahead of time from coat hangers. You will have to cut the hangers and straighten them and then show the kids how to sand the paint off and scrub them. You can also use bamboo skewers or wooden ones, but you must soak them in water for about an hour to prevent their catching fire on the grill. Cover the handles with foil to make them easier to turn. You can assign this chore to one of the kids.

Ending the Evening

Since you have turned to the kids to help plan, cook and serve the barbecue party, do not forget to include them in the cleanup as well. They can dismantle the decorations and collect trash while you tend to the grill. Once the yard or park is cleaned up, the kids can also help you with the dishes and kitchen chores. If the grill is cool, one of them can scour off the grate with a brush, soap and water and a hose. This barbeque endeavor has allowed you to present lessons on art, math and cooking, and it follows that you need to make clear that cleanup is part of having a party. Most kids are eager to help, especially if they can look forward to catching fireflies afterward before settling down to sing some songs before bed.

Resources

www.girlsatthegrill.com/fun/kids.asp

This Website has been designed to teach kids about grilling. You can download a Grilling Activity Book that includes instructions for decorating a menu, making a paper kebab and cooking unusual recipes.

Cooking on a Stick (Activities for Kids), (Gibbs, Smith Publisher, 2000).

This book tells everything you need to know about campfire cooking, including building a fire, creating simple recipes and cooking on a grill.

15

Make a Mess: Papier-Mâché

The secret to a successful papier-mâché experience is planning. Select a day when you have time to supervise and choose a place that is easily cleaned. Making papier-mâché outdoors on a picnic table or plastic-covered card table is ideal. If you are working inside, cover all surfaces with plastic or layers of old newspapers. This makes cleanup simple and fast.

Making Papier-Mâché

Papier-mâché is a simple combination of strips of paper–newspaper, brown craft paper, plain white copy paper or even paper towels–and some form of a paste. Most people use newspaper because it is inexpensive. However, if your kids are going to paint the final object, you may want to use white copy paper as the last layer; it requires much less paint to cover white paper.

There are several ways to make papier-mâché paste:

- Make a solution of 3/4 part white glue to 1/4 part water (if you are using a heavy, thick white glue, try half and half proportions).
- Stir together one part white flour to one part water. Mix thoroughly to eliminate lumps.
- Mix together one part white flour to five parts water. Boil about three minutes and let cool.

This third method in which you boil the solution is the cheapest and produces the smoothest paste. You can get the same smooth result, however, by simply using liquid starch. The final appearance of the paper is smooth and clear, which is what you want if you are using colored or decorated paper.

Tips to Remember

Here are some helpful hints about making papier-mâché objects:

- Consider humidity. If you live in a humid climate, add less water (up to one quarter less) to your paste.

- Add salt (one or two tablespoons) to your paste to prevent mold.
- Allow the project to dry completely before adding new layers of paper or painting.
- Never cover the project with more than four layers of paper per application period. If you need a more solid end result, continue to cover, four layers at a time, but allow the paper to dry completely between applications.
- Make only the amount of paste that you need for a project since unused paste tends to spoil. You may even want to start fresh with every application of paper since it may take some time for the paper to dry between applications.

Papier-Mâché Projects

The basic procedure for making papier-mâché objects is to tear up 8 to 10 newspaper pages into one- by six-inch strips. Briefly soak the strips in the paste solution and then run the strips between two fingers to strip off any excess paste. Lay each strip carefully, one by one, on the underlying structure applying no more than four layers deep per application period. Smooth out the paper with your hands and wipe off unnecessary paste. Allow it to dry completely and then reapply more strips to complete the project. It is extremely important that each layer dry thoroughly before more strips are added.

Before you start any project, set out everything you will need. Cover the working area with large sheets of newspaper and then a plastic sheet or waxed paper. Tear up the paper you plan to use into strips, make the paste and assemble all the parts your project requires. Be sure you have a place to store the projects while they dry.

Papier-Mâché Piñata

You will need a large balloon and string along with the papier-mâché and decorating materials.

Blow up a large balloon and tie it closed. The balloon may be hard to hold on to while you are layering the paper strips, so you can have two children work together or anchor the balloon in a bowl covered with plastic wrap.

Dip the paper strips into the paste and smooth them over the balloon. Cover the balloon completely except for a small hole at the top to pull out the balloon later and fill the piñata. Allow the layer to dry and then apply two or three more layers. Again, allow the paper to dry.

When the paper is dry, pop the balloon and remove it through the hole in the top. You can now paint and decorate the piñata and hang streamers or ribbons from the bottom. When you are ready to hang the piñata, push four small holes at even intervals around the hole in the top. Pull twine or string through the holes and gather together into a knot at the top. Tie a string to the knot; be sure the string is long enough for the kids to reach the piñata after you hang it up.

Papier-Mâché Puppet

You will need a balloon, a 2-foot long 1/2-inch dowel rod, masking tape, glue and construction paper or yarn.

Blow up a balloon and knot it closed. Cover the entire balloon with papier-mâché strips, leaving a small opening around the knot at the bottom. Allow it to dry completely.

Fashion a nose from papier-mâché strips and press onto the covered balloon. Once the nose is dry, pop the balloon at the knot and pull it out. Slide the dowel rod through the hole in the bottom and use masking tape to anchor it. Add another layer of papier-mâché strips, being careful to cover over the tape at the bottom.

When the object is dry, paint a face and glue on construction paper or yarn hair.

Papier-Mâché Mask

You will need poster board or cardboard and string as well as the papier-mâché and decorating materials.

Begin by asking each child to draw a picture of the mask he or she would like to wear. Then transfer the drawings or redraw onto poster board or cardboard. Cut out the drawn masks, layer them with papier-mâché strips and allow them to dry. Before applying additional strips, cut out holes for eyes, nose and mouth if desired. Poke a hole on either side of the mask to attach a string so that the mask can be worn.

Decorating the mask is the most fun. Provide lots of different supplies such beads, fabric, laces, ribbons and construction paper including glue and let your kids use their imaginations.

This project is a good opportunity to combine imaginative play with a craft activity. Have the kids write a play before they make the masks and then design the masks to fit the story line. After they finish the masks, they can perform the play.

Papier-Mâché Volcano

You will need a foil pie pan or square piece of heavy-duty cardboard for the base, an empty plastic drink bottle and masking tape as well as the papier-mâché and decorating materials.

Place the plastic bottle upright into the center of the pan or cardboard base. Anchor strips of masking tape from the top of the bottle downward and outward toward the edges of the cardboard. Apply papier-mâché strips between the masking tape from the top of the bottle to the edges of the cardboard. Allow to dry completely. Once the object has dried, preferably overnight, paint and decorate to look like a mountain.

A papier-mâché volcano is rather boring unless it erupts like a real volcano. Fortunately, that is easy to do. Pour one cup of vinegar into the top of the volcano (into the plastic bottle) and add a few drops of both red and yellow food coloring. When you are ready, quickly drop four tablespoons of baking soda into the top of the volcano. Stand back and watch.

In addition to adding a little excitement to the project, the vinegar-baking soda step affords an opportunity to teach a science lesson about chemical reactions. For a good explanation of the science behind this reaction, visit *http://pbskids. org/zoom/activities/sci/bakingsodabubbles.html*.

Making Gifts

If your kids enjoy making papier-mâché objects and become proficient at handling the materials, you might want to suggest they consider making some holiday gifts from papier-mâché. It is fairly easy to mold papier-mâché over inverted bowls to make baskets and decorative bowls to give as gifts. The final creation can be varnished to seal the object and add to its strength. The result is a container than can hold mail, silk flowers or small decorative objects. And you have a head start on holiday shopping.

Resources

www.sitesforparents.com/index.html

> This Website offers lesson plans, worksheets, links and activities for parents and teachers.

Papier Mâché, (Kids Can Press).

> This book is directed toward beginners and includes a supply list, specific project ideas and painting and decorating tips.

Papier Mâché for Kids, (Firefly Books, 1991).

> This is a how-to book for kids.

16

Dinosaurs

Dinosaurs fascinate kids. They like to hear about dinosaurs, to read about them, and to learn about them as well. This means that you will have a captive audience as soon as you mention the topic.

Before you start any hands-on activities about dinosaurs, you and the children will need to make a trip to the library. Tell the kids you want them to locate interesting books about dinosaurs, including texts with pictures and descriptions of dinosaurs' habitats. Have someone look up dinosaurs in various encyclopedias–if the information is pertinent, have them photocopy the pages. You should also take out as many books as you can so that all of you can read about dinosaurs at home. Look for books and information that are suitable for the age levels of your kids.

Incidentally, a bonus here is the opportunity to teach your kids how to use the library. Enlist the librarian to help. After all, knowing everything about a topic is not necessarily a sign of high intelligence; rather, knowing where to find the information is the key to becoming informed.

After you have collected what you need from the library, send your kids to the Internet to search for dinosaurs. Again, tell them to look for illustrations and information about all types of dinosaurs. Print out what you can use and sort through the information to eliminate duplications and to create a cohesive, yet comprehensive, activity plan. There is enough information about dinosaurs–and enough interest on your kids' part–to turn this into a summer-long project that you can return to when you need something to occupy the kids.

Dinosaur Projects

Creating dinosaur projects keep kids busy for hours. And there is a dinosaur activity that is suitable for every age and every ability.

Dinosaur Habitat

A good place to begin, especially for older kids, is construction of a dinosaur habitat. Ask the kids to go to their library resources and to Internet sites in order to learn about where dinosaurs dwelled and how they lived. Meanwhile, you gather the supplies you will need. Supplies include a shallow cardboard box, brown play dough (see Chapter 3 for a recipe for homemade play dough), paints, rocks, blue liquid glue, an empty food can or bottle and plastic toy plants and dinosaurs (available at discount shops or at dollar stores).

1. Start with the cardboard box. The bottom from a case of bottled water or carton of soft drinks is ideal, or you can cut the bottom from a regular cardboard container.
2. Have the kids paint the interior of the box green. Ask the kids if they want to paint other background features before going any further.
3. To form hills and terrain, the kids can use food coloring to dye play dough brown or use cocoa. Scatter rocks around to add interest.
4. The blue liquid glue creates colorful watering holes and streams.
5. When the habitat is finished and dry, the children can position their dinosaurs in place.

Dinosaur Diorama

A dinosaur diorama may be a better activity for younger kids. This is simply a scene inside a box, like a shoe box or any box that can be placed on its side to create a window to hold a scene.

To start, ask the kids to cover the outside of the box with construction paper of their choice and glue it in place. If the interior of the box is a dark color, line the box with white paper, cut the paper to fit the box and glue it into place. Have the kids decorate the inside of the box with markers or crayons to recreate a dinosaurs' environment. If you and the kids recall from your research, the Earth was warm and volcanoes were evident during the time that dinosaurs lived– these facts will help you decide how to decorate the diorama. Be sure to have the kids draw a picture of a volcano on the back wall.

Ask the kids to trace or draw pictures of dinosaurs and trees on construction paper and then cut out the figures. Glue them to thin cardboard (an empty cereal box works well), leaving enough extra cardboard at the bottom to fold and glue into standing positions in the diorama. If you want plants to look different from animals, use green and brown pipe cleaners for plant shapes. If your kids have made flying dinosaurs, you can hang them from the inside top of the box with tape or string.

Dinosaur Dig

You can find out if your kids may be future paleontologists (scientists who find and study ancient fossils) by doing one or both of the following activities.

Save and clean some chicken or turkeys bones from dinner. Place each bone into a container into which you and the kids have packed wet sand. Carefully remove each bone from the sand and then pour Plaster of Paris into the imprint left behind. When the Plastic of Paris hardens, remove the fossil from the sand and ask the children to label the fossil and mount it on poster board to display.

Or take plastic toy dinosaurs, the larger the better, and press parts of their bodies into containers of wet sand. Remove the toys and pour Plaster of Paris into each impression. When the fossils dry, ask the kids to remove each plaster fossil, brush off the sand with small dry paintbrushes and label them. Later, each child can describe to the family each fossil and its dinosaur.

Making Dinosaurs

You can make a couple of types of dinosaurs depending on the ages and interests of your kids. You can start by asking the kids to write a short puppet play about dinosaurs and then help them make the puppets to enact the play. Stick puppets work well. Have the kids draw and color the dinosaur characters and then glue them to Popsicle™ sticks or paint-stirring sticks. Turn a table on its side for a stage and sit back to enjoy the play.

Preschool-age kids like to make stuffed dinosaurs. Find some illustrations of dinosaurs and enlarge them on the library's copy machine. Show the kids how to trace around the dinosaur shape to make two identical tracings on two pieces of heavy paper. Have the kids cut out the shapes, decorate them and color the body. Then you or an older child can staple the shapes together, leaving a hole large enough to stuff the dinosaur. The kids can stuff the shapes with newspaper or tissue paper. When they see the dinosaur's head in its final form, the kids can add facial features and complete the decorating. You finish the form by stapling shut the hole through which they stuffed the shape.

Making Dinosaur Eggs

You and your children can turn out a batch of dinosaur eggs for fun or for party decorations. There are two ways to do this:

1. Get together balloons, one for each egg, a batch of papier-mâché (see Chapter 15), tempera paints and markers.
2. Insert a tiny plastic toy dinosaur into each balloon.

3. Blow up each balloon and tie it shut.

4. Cover the balloons with papier-mâché and allow to dry.

5. Pop and remove the balloons and let the kids paint the eggs.

Later the kids can hatch their eggs to find a baby dinosaur–this is especially fun at a party.

Making Dinosaur Hats

This is an easy project similar to making dinosaur eggs.

1. Use a blown-up balloon to mold the hat. Work on the balloon sideways because dinosaurs generally had long heads.

2. Apply three layers of papier-mâché strips onto the top half of the balloon.

3. Allow the papier-mâché to dry for several days.

4. When the form is dry, pop the balloon, paint and decorate. The kids can glue on horns, beaks, teeth or other parts made from paper, Styrofoam, egg cartons or cardboard. Paint on some eyes, nostrils or scales and allow to dry.

5. The last step is to punch holes with a paper punch into each side and attach a chin strap of string, shoelace or elastic.

Resources

The Simon and Schuster Encyclopedia of Dinosaurs and Prehistoric Creatures, (Simon and Schuster, 1999).

This richly illustrated book discusses in detail more than 500 million years of evolution including descriptions of dinosaurs, their habitats, their diets and their living conditions. An excellent sourcebook.

National Geographic Dinosaurs, (National Geographic Children's Books, 2001).

This book is a great resource with excellent illustrations.

www.enchantedlearning.com/subjects/dinosaurs/toc.shtml

This Website is a good source of online activities involving dinosaurs.

Dazzle the Dinosaur, (North-South, 2000).

This is a fantasy story about a dinosaur, written for children between the ages of four and eight.

Dinosaurs Alive!, (Random House, 2001).

This book introduces dinosaurs in an easy-to-read format (geared toward children from grades two to four) and includes excellent illustrations.

Puppet Show

Making puppets and performing puppet shows are wonderful ways to occupy children who need something to do on rainy days. All you need is some basic craft supplies and your children's imaginations to create puppets and puppet theaters that your kids can return to all summer long.

Gathering Supplies

Having children means you probably have already stocked up on craft supplies for them to use. Rummage through your supplies to find ideas for constructing puppets and puppet theaters. You can also visit craft stores (looks for sales or coupons) or save sewing scraps, outgrown clothing (socks or T-shirts), leftover workshop materials or cardboard boxes. Look around the kitchen for paper bags, paper plates, drinking straws, Popsicle™ sticks or food wrappers. And do not forget to include glue, paint, stickers and markers.

Making Puppets

When you begin to make puppets, ask your kids to select what type of puppets they want to make or what kind of show they want to perform since that may determine the types of puppets to construct. You can make several varieties of hand puppets, stick puppets or string marionettes. Keep in mind, too, the kind of puppet theater you plan to build and the number of kids participating. Here are a few suggestions for each kind of puppet.

Hand Puppets

The easiest hand puppets are fashioned from old socks, gloves, paper plates or paper bags.

Sock Puppets

To create a basic sock puppet:

> 1. Fit each sock to the child's hand and mark eyes, nose and mouth.

2. Cut a circle of cardboard from a cereal box or similar container and fold it in half.

3. Insert the cardboard into the toe of the sock and push it curved side out to the end of the toe to create a mouth. If the cardboard is too large, trim it to fit the sock. The child should place his four fingers on the top of the cardboard circle and the thumb on the bottom.

4. If you want, you can trim away the cloth around the mouthpiece leaving a one-half-inch cut that will allow you to glue both pieces of the cloth onto the cardboard mouthpiece.

You now have a basic sock puppet you can decorate or mark to create specific creatures or personalities. Let each kid decide how he wants to finish the puppet or encourage a group of children to create a cast of characters for their own play or performance. For example, to make a caterpillar sock puppet:

1. Take a sock and mark the location of the eyes and nose while the sock is on the child's hand.

2. Have the child pull the sock off and glue two large pompons (or cotton balls) for eyes and a small pompon for a nose onto the sock. You can also use buttons.

3. Think about gluing small pompons or cotton balls along the sides of the sock to create feet.

4. Paint the tips of the feet with permanent ink markers.

5. If you want, glue wiggly eyes from the craft store onto the eyes' pompons.

6. Cut a pipe cleaner in half and poke each half through the sock's toe to construct antennae.

7. Finally, glue on a fabric scrap of a contrasting color for the tongue.

Glove Puppets

Glove puppets are a combination of sock and stick puppets. You will need cotton garden gloves, various craft items and scraps and some kind of dowel rod or sturdy stick like a pencil or wooden spoon.

You can make glove puppets in one of two ways. One way to make a glove puppet is to stuff all of the glove fingers with quilt batting or clean rags, tying off the fingers with string or yarn where the fingers meet the hand of the glove. The kids can decorate each finger as a separate figure by gluing on fabric, beads, pompons or feathers. Or they can use the fingers as antennae or as a headpiece. To do so, they will need to stuff batting into the hand of the glove to fashion a body and then tie off the cuff of the glove around a dowel rod or stick.

Another way to make a glove puppet is to create an animal from the entire glove. For example, poke the thumb of the glove to the inside. Then fold the index and pinky finger over to form arms and glue in place. You can also glue an object onto the glove between the arms of the creature. The middle two fingers can become ears (for instance, rabbit ears or donkey ears). Decorate the glove with fabric scraps, buttons, ribbons or cotton balls. Use markers to draw directly onto the glove. When you have finished decorating the glove, stuff it with batting or rags and tie the cuff around a rod or stick. As the kids create their puppet story or puppet show, help them think of ways to complete their figure by using the stuffed-in thumb. Perhaps they can insert a small party umbrella (used with certain drinks) into the thumb opening. Encourage them to be creative.

Paper Plate Stick Puppets

For example, make some flower puppets by gluing a CD to a paper plate, the edge of which has been trimmed into petals. Once you have decorated the flower (there are felt-tip markers that will write on CDs), glue it to either a rod or the sole of an old sock. The kids can use it as a stick puppet or slip their hands into the sock to activate the flower.

Your kids can make an elephant puppet by coloring a paper plate gray and cutting out a circle on the plate where the trunk would be. Glue a Popsicle™ stick to the back of the plate to control the puppet and instruct the kids to slip their finger or arm through the hole in the plate to represent the trunk.

To make a butterfly puppet, fold a paper plate in half. Using a second plate, cut a one-inch strip from the middle of the plate and throw away the strip. Take each of the half plates you just cut out and place them onto the first folded plate, taping around the round outside edges only. You have just made two pockets in which you can insert your fingers to control the puppet. Draw a butterfly on the plates and poke two holes at the top through which you can slip pipe cleaner antennae. Insert your fingers into the pockets and make the butterfly flap its wings.

Paper plate and drinking straw puppets are easy enough and fast enough to make that even very young kids can create their own puppets. Have the kids draw an outline of the creature they want on the plate such as a cat, dog, rabbit or fish and then cut out the silhouette of the creature. They can use construction paper, yarn, feathers or just markers to decorate. Finally, tape a drinking straw to the back of the paper plate.

Marionettes

Making a marionette is not as difficult as you might think, and you can use objects that you have around the house. You will need some lightweight cardboard (a cereal box is fine), yarn, construction paper, bottle caps and a dowel rod or a small stick.

1. For heads and bodies, cut off the corners from an empty cereal box (the box can serve as the puppet body). Have the kids decorate these pieces before assembling them (as various body parts) into the puppet.
2. Knot three pieces of yarn at one end and braid them.
3. Punch a hole through the puppet head and body and pull the unknotted end of the braid through first one hole and then the other. Tie the loose ends of the braid into knots.
4. Again braid three yarn strands for legs and punch holes in either side of the body to pull the legs through.
5. Glue bottles caps on the bottom for feet (bottle caps make satisfying clicking noises when the puppet walks).
6. Finally, knot the ends of two separate pieces of yarn (the length depends on the child's height) and pull the unknotted ends through holes you have poked in the head and body. Tie the unknotted ends to a dowel rod or a stick. The marionette is now ready for the stage.

Building a Puppet Stage

1. Find a large cardboard box; cut a rectangular flap out of the bottom, folding down the flap to form a shelf at the bottom.
2. Ask the kids to paint and/or decorate the outside of the theater.
3. When the outside is decorated, staple or glue a piece of fabric across the inside of the back of the box.
4. Place the box, open front facing outward, on a table.
5. When the puppet show begins, the kids sit on the floor behind the table and reach in front of the fabric backing to the shelf.

For a marionette show, turn a card table on its side or use a large square board to form the back of a stage. The kids stand behind the table and work the marionettes from above.

Resources

http://fun.familyeducation.com/holidays-and-celebrations/gifts/45245.html

This Website features instructions for making all kinds of puppets.

http://familycrafts.about.com/cs/puppets/a/blpbpuppet.htm

This Website describes various puppets suitable for all ages.

Unplugged Family Fun Activities, (Perseus Book Group, Inc., 2005).

As its title implies, this book provides ideas for family activities that pull the kids away from the computer and TV.

18

Indoor Games with Tape

An indoor day during a long summer can be a challenge. Whether it is too hot, too rainy or too smoggy, the day forces everyone inside to occupy themselves with indoor activities. If you and your kids want a break from crafts, painting, reading and other indoor activities, suggest a tape day. Activities with tape can range from something as simple as creating sculptures from tape to wrapping a mummy while learning about ancient Egypt.

A word about cost. While tape in general–that is, Scotch®, masking, duct, electrical and adhesive tape–is not too expensive, it is not free, either. Check weekly ads occurring at your local hardware store, grocery store, drugstore or variety store for sales or two-for-one specials and then stock up. Store your kids' tape separately from your own toolbox and make it clear that the kids are to use only their own tape. It is irritating to reach for duct tape during a household repair and find it gone.

Activities with Tape

Once you have accumulated a supply of tape, you are ready to occupy the kids with some indoor activities using it. Here are some suggestions for those long days indoors.

Old Standbys

These games are very familiar and are often played outside. But they can be adapted to indoor play, especially if you have a large space such as a basement or a garage.

If you have enough space, you and the kids can set up a playing field that includes three games. In the first game, have the kids lay out a tic-tac-toe board with tape. They can play the game with buttons or rocks in one of two ways: either play as usual in which a player tries to get his or her three buttons in a row or play the game the opposite way in which each player tries NOT to get three of his buttons in a row. In the first way, the player with three in a row wins; in the second way, the player with three in a row loses.

In the second game, instruct the children to use tape to lay out a four-square field. Start by creating one large square measuring 12 feet by 12 feet with tape. Divide this square with tape into four equal squares measuring six feet by six feet. Number the squares one through four using tape or taping down marked scraps of paper. One player occupies each square and the player in square #1 begins by bouncing a kickball in his square once and then hitting it toward one of the other squares. Play continues until a player hits the ball or is hit by the ball before it bounces in his square, does not hit the ball before it bounces twice or hits the ball out of bounds. The player who commits one of these errors moves to the lowest ranking square (square #4) while the others move forward one square. If there are more than four players, the player who is out goes to the end of a waiting line of players.

The third game is a favorite tape game. Use masking tape to mark off a hopscotch board into eight numbered sections. Supply each player with a marker and instruct the first player to stand behind a taped-down starting line to toss his marker into square #1. Player #1 hops over square #1 to square #2 and onward to square #8 at which point he turns and hops back to square #2 where, standing on one foot, the player picks up the marker from square #1. Play continues by tossing the marker into successive squares, hopping and then retrieving the marker. The players must hop on one foot except when two squares lie side by side and must hop over any square where there is a marker. A player is out if the marker fails to land on the correct square, the hopper loses his balance and puts a foot or a hand down to balance, the hopper steps into a square where there is a maker or the hopper places two feet in one box. At that point the player who is out places a marker where he will resume playing on the next turn.

Tape Relay Race

Mark off a playing field by taping a starting line and a finishing line. Have the kids team up in pairs and use masking tape to tape one player's right arm to the other player's left leg and the second player's left arm to the first player's right leg. Blow a whistle or clap your hands and the players race to the finish line and back. The first team to make it to both lines wins.

Wrapped Gift Game

The goal of this game is to open a wrapped gift while wearing a coat, a hat, a scarf and oven mitts. First, have an older child place a small gift, such as a cookie or candy, into a small box. The wrapper should wrap the box and place it into a succession of larger and larger boxes, wrapping each box as he goes. The wrapper should use ample amounts of tape–preferably duct tape–to wrap the boxes and the final package. This should be done in secret.

Supply a pair of dice and a cookie sheet or smooth board on which to roll the dice. Place the coat, the hat, the scarf and oven mitts on the floor next to the cookie sheet. Ask another child to choose a number between one and ten. Each player then gets one roll of the dice before passing it on to the next player. When someone rolls the number selected, he must put on all the clothes (coat, hat, scarf and oven mitts) and try to unwrap the taped package. This player can keep trying to unwrap the package until another player rolls the selected number. At that point, the first player must take off the outer clothes and hand them over to the new player. You can elect to pause the game until the transfer takes place, or you can allow players to continue to roll the dice as the transfer takes place. The first person to unwrap the final package within the limits is the winner.

Making a Costume

Suggest that your kids compete in a fashion show. Furnish tape and plenty of newspapers. In order to select a panel of judges, have the kids count off; then divide the remaining kids into as many teams as you want. Tell each team to select a costume they want to design and construct from tape and newspapers. Also remind them to select one member to be the model.

Your role in this game is to remain in the background and supply newspapers. Encourage the kids to be as creative as possible while ensuring that their final fashions are sturdy as well as attractive. This is not necessarily a game for girls only; boys can design monster costumes or robots. You could even suggest that each team try to stump the other teams about the identity of the person or creature who would wear their design.

Mummy Wrap

Similar to the costume designing contest, the mummy wrap involves wrapping a child in toilet paper to resemble a mummy. Divide the group into teams of four kids each, and allow each child to draw a job from a hat. One of the four will draw to be the mummy while the others are wrappers.

You and the kids decide the rules of the game. Is the winner going to be the team that wraps their mummy faster than the other teams or the team that does the best job? Once you and the kids have set the ground rules (including keeping the mummy's eyes, nose and mouth uncovered and not flinging rolls of toilet paper around the room), hand out three rolls of toilet paper to each team along with a roll of masking tape. If your kids are especially active, try duct tape. You can then stand on the sidelines with a timer and a pair of scissors to rescue the mummies.

Neighborhood Map

Challenge your kids to lay out a map of your neighborhood from memory, using tape on a smooth floor or carpet. Start with your home and move in all four directions. The kids can use tape to lay out streets, buildings, parks and other features. If they want, they can tape down colored paper to fill in their map; for example, green construction paper for parks or grassy areas. When the kids have finished the map, ask them to take a look at the layout and decide how they could improve the neighborhood. They can then either tape out a new, improved neighborhood if you have the floor space or add changes to the existing map.

Miniature Golf

The object of this game is to play a game of miniature golf by blowing a ping pong ball through a golf course in the least number of puffs.

In addition to two ping pong balls and a smooth floor or carpet, you will need tape, small boxes, empty toilet paper tubes or empty paper towel tubes, scraps of cardboard and other assorted objects to construct the course. Let your kids use their imaginations in designing each hole. One hole can be on the floor level at the end of a small cardboard box taped to the floor with a semicircle cut from the bottom of two sides. For another hole, tape a ramp made from a cardboard scrap and two paper towel tubes to guide the ball up the ramp to a box resting on top of a stack of magazines. Cut a hole into the top of the box to catch the ball and then cut a flap in the bottom of the box to direct the ball to the next hole. Have the kids go on to design at least nine holes that can be taped together to form a course. Encourage your kids to devise a way to make the course moveable so that they can continue to play miniature golf all summer long.

Resources

Creativity for Kids: Tape Crazy, (Faber-Castell/Creativity For Kids).

This is a kit that includes seven spools of printed tapes in mini-tape dispensers and matching stickers for kids to use to decorate different objects.

Totally Tape, (Klutz Press).

This book includes four rolls of paper tape along with pages and projects to tape. This spiral-bound activity book can be used on road trips as well as indoors.

19

Starting an Aquarium

Setting up an aquarium is not an inexpensive undertaking. The proper equipment, not to mention the cost of the fish, can be costly. Most experts advise against cheap package deals that imply you can start an aquarium for a few dollars. Instead, you should research what is needed for a successful aquarium before you commit to the idea. This, of course, means that you must conduct your research before even mentioning the idea to the kids.

What You Will Need

You will need the following items:

- A tank, preferably larger rather than smaller.
  A 20-gallon aquarium is about right. Choose an oblong tank, one that is longer and shorter, rather than one that is tall and slender. The oblong tank provides more swimming area and more surface area for air exchange.
- A stand to hold the tank.
  Tanks are heavy–allow a generous 10 pounds for each gallon of water– so you must have something that will support that weight.

Weight of Filled Tanks		
Aquarium size (Glass)	L x W x H	Filled Weight
10 gallon	20" x 10" x 12"	111 pounds
15 gallon	24" x 12" x 12"	170 pounds
20 gallons	30" x 12" x 12"	225 pounds
30 gallons	36" x 18" x 12"	348 pounds
40 gallons	48" x 12" x 16"	455 pounds
50 gallons	36" x 18" x 19"	600 pounds

- A cover or lid, generally combined with a light.

  The lid prevents the fish from jumping out, the cat from jumping in, the light from getting wet and the water from evaporating too quickly. Plastic lids are cheaper, lighter and less breakable. Glass lids allow more light into the tank and are easier to clean. The best bulb for the light is a fluorescent one because it is cooler and costs less to operate.

- A filtration system.

  This is important. The size of the filter must match the size of the tank, and you should select a filter with a flow rate that filters all of the water in your tank at least four times an hour. Therefore, a 20-gallon tank must have a filter with a flow rate of at least 80 gallons per hour.

- A heater.

  In general, fish require a water temperature of about 77 degrees Fahrenheit. If your home's temperature is not consistently 77 degrees F, you will need a heater. A rule of thumb is a heater that uses five watts per gallon for small tanks and three watts per gallon for larger tanks.

- A thermometer.

  Liquid crystal stick-on thermometers are fine.

- A net.

  In fact, two nets—it is easier to catch fish using two nets.

- Water conditioner.

  Water must be dechlorinated before fish are added. Get a water conditioner that eliminates chlorine, ammonia and heavy metals.

- Test kits.

  You need to test water in new tanks as well as in tanks that have undergone changes. Look for kits that test ammonia, nitrite and pH.

- A siphon.

  Basic maintenance requires that you vacuum the gravel in the tank for waste material and change part of the water on a regular basis.

- An algae scrubber.

  Algae is a given in an aquarium so periodically you will need to scrub the inside walls of the tank.

- A water bucket with a label stating that it is to be used for fish only.

Setting Up the Tank

When you arrive at the aquarium shop, outline your requirements to the sales clerk and ask for advice as you begin to gather what you need. You should have your list (from the paragraphs above) as a starting point, but you also want to discuss plants, other decorations and gravel with the clerk. Ask about the amount of gravel you need and how to buy fish food. Meanwhile, the kids will be standing at the fish tanks deciding which ones they like. This is the time to tell the kids that they will have to set up the tank at home and leave it for a few days before purchasing fish so that the water temperature can stabilize and water toxins, such as chlorine, can dissolve.

Once you are home, decide where the tank should go, but do not set it near a heating or cooling source or in direct sunlight because this can cause the water temperature to fluctuate. Ask the kids to rinse everything that is going into the tank with tap water, including the inside of the tank–this is also the time to test for leaks in the tank. Do not use any detergents or cleaning solutions because they may leave residue that is harmful to the fish. Use your special fish bucket to add water.

Buying Fish

When you and the kids go back to the pet store to buy fish, ask about the source of the fish. Only buy fish that have been raised on fish farms for the pet trade. Ask the clerk how to select fish that will get along with each other and thrive in your tank. The kids, of course, can select their favorites, but be certain the fish are compatible before buying them. You do not want to wake up one morning and find that an aggressive fish has dispatched all of his tank mates.

How many fish can your tank hold? The basic rule is one inch of fish per gallon of water. But full-bodied fish require more space and tall slender tanks provides less air exchange than long shorter ones. The best approach is to populate your tank with small-bodied fish that are less than an inch long.

When you bring home your new fish, float the plastic travel bag containing the fish in the aquarium for about 10 minutes to allow the water temperatures in both environments to equalize. Then open the bag and add tank water to the bag until the water volume in the bag doubles. Wait about 5 minutes and then, using a net, scoop the fish out of the bag and into the tank. Do not add the bag's water to your tank as it may contaminate the tank water.

Care and Maintenance

These are the tasks that the children can assume, especially if they are older. When it comes to ongoing care, you can delegate chores according to a child's age and ability. Very young kids can feed the fish, taking care not to overfeed, and older kids can be responsible for cleaning the tank and testing the water.

Feeding the Fish

If you and the children have set up the tank to provide a safe sanctuary for the fish, you are ready to select fish food. Again, rely on the pet store clerk to advise you about the eating habits of your fish including what they eat, when they eat, and where they eat. Some eat at night (turn off the tank light when you go to bed), some eat on the water's surface and some eat at the bottom at gravel level. Bottom feeders need food that sinks.

It is important to retain nutritional value—flake food especially becomes stale quickly. So, do not buy more food than you can use in a few weeks. Ask the kids to set up a timeline or calendar next to the tank noting the purchase date of fish food, so you can replace it when it becomes stale. Aim for variety as well; combine dry foods with frozen foods or fresh to ensure a balanced diet.

Cleaning the Tank

Explain that it is not necessary to empty the tank and take it apart to clean. In fact, taking the tank apart eliminates beneficial bacterial colonies that break down the wastes produced by the fish in the water. Instead, once a month remove about one third of the water and replace it with treated and tested tap water at the same temperature as the water in the tank.

Clean the filter a week or two after you clean the tank. This allows the beneficial bacteria in the filter to replenish the bacteria you removed when you cleaned the tank. You and the kids can establish a 2-week cleaning cycle for the tank and the filter and note it on the same calendar that the kids have made for buying fish food. Each week you can clean the algae away and siphon off debris from the gravel. Then clean the filter and replace part of the water once a month. As you will soon learn, caring for fish and a tank is not a once-in-a-while task. Still, the view into a microcosm of the marine world is worth the effort.

Resources

www.aquariumfish.net/information/fish_for_children.htm

This Website provides detailed guidelines to buying fish. The information is geared toward parents and kids.

101 Essential Tips: Aquarium Fish, (DK Adult, 2004).

This is an illustrated guide to choosing and caring for aquarium fish with detailed information on regulating aquarium conditions. There is also specific information about freshwater, coldwater and marine tropical fish.

A Simple Guide to Freshwater Aquariums, (TFH Publications, 2001).

This book provides complete information about selecting equipment, fish and plants.

Macmillan Book of the Marine Aquarium, (Simon and Schuster, 1993).

This book discusses equipment and the needs of individual fish.

Building
Mobiles

A mobile is a hanging sculpture that consists of objects attached to rods that are balanced and suspended in midair and set in motion by air currents. While your kids may think building a mobile sounds difficult to do, they are probably familiar with the art form, since one of the most popular baby toys is a colorful mobile suspended above a crib. Nevertheless, there is an art to assembling a mobile, and your kids may find it engrossing to tackle the project.

The basic secret is to start from the bottom and work to the top. First, have your kids design the mobile in its final form on paper. Then collect the components, including the small hanging objects and the rods. Arrange all the pieces out on a large piece of paper in its final design. Show the kids how to draw lines connecting the bottom end pieces.

The next step is to wire or attach all the end pieces first and then attach all the middle systems together. Connect the middle systems to the top bar and hang the sculpture.

This sounds simple, but remember to advise the kids that they will have to tinker with the assembled sculpture in order to achieve a final balance of all the components.

Supplies

Challenge the kids to use their own ingenuity to find mobile components around the house. Raid the junk drawer in the kitchen or garage. Coat hangers make good rods. Thread, string, cardboard, beads, small jewelry, buttons and other small items can be hung from the rods. You probably can also find all the craft supplies you need around the house–unless you want to work with wire, in which case you will need some needle nose pliers.

Very young children not yet adept with scissors, wire and pliers can construct a simple mobile using drinking straws for the rods, paper clips (singly or hooked together at different lengths) slid onto the straws (in lieu of wires or threads) and construction paper cutouts (such as butterflies or Valentine hearts) as the objects attached to the ends of the paper clips.

Mobile Patterns

Here are a couple of mobile designs for you and the kids to try. Emphasize, however, that the fun of making mobiles is developing your own designs, so encourage individual work after the kid have made one of the mobiles here.

Solar System Mobile

You may have to start with a brief lesson about the solar system, including a discussion about why Pluto is no longer classified as a planet. See Resources at the end of this chapter.

What you need:

- A 12-inch-diameter round cardboard from a frozen pizza box (or cut a circle from a cardboard box)
- Additional cardboard boxes
- Black construction paper (or flat black spray paint)
- A compass (for creating circles)
- A pair of scissors
- Glitter–any colors you like
- White glue
- A small paintbrush
- Thread (black is best) or fine nylon fishing line
- A small, four-holed button
- A large, sturdy sewing needle
- Sixteen very small beads, black is best (optional)

First, make the planets by cutting cardboard into different-sized circles. For this your kids may need to do some research so that they can learn the relative size of the different planets. The range in size of the Sun relative to the size of the planets is too large to represent accurately, so simply make the Sun the largest (around two-inches in diameter) and scale down from there–make Jupiter, Saturn, Uranus and Neptune a little smaller than the Sun and the rest of the plants much smaller than the second level. Saturn has rings, so include these in the cutout.

Use the cardboard cutouts of the planets as patterns to cut out construction paper to cover both sides of each planet. Glue the paper to the planets and encourage the kids to decorate to make each planet look distinctive. Use the paintbrush to spread glue thinly on one side of each planet. Sprinkle one or two colors of glitter on each, and when the first side has dried, turn the planets over and decorate the other sides. Be sure to leave them lying flat until the glue is completely dry.

Make the frame for the mobile by covering the 12-inch round cardboard cutout with black construction paper or flat black spray paint. Make three pencil marks equally spaced around the edge of the circle, about one-inch in from the edge.

Find the center of this frame by drawing two pencil lines, one from top to bottom and the other from side to side. Where the lines intersect is the center of the circle and the position of the Sun. Using a compass, draw circles (the orbits of the planets) around the center of the cardboard. The first four planets are close to the Sun, and then there is a gap before the orbits of the last four planets. Take the points of a pair of scissors or a large nail and punch a hole in the center of the cardboard where the Sun will hang and then punch a hole in each orbit from which a planet will hang.

Cut a length of thread about two feet long. Thread the needle and either tie a fat knot in the end or tie a small bead to the end (include only one strand of thread). Poke the needle through one of the pencil marks on the edge of the cardboard circle. Pull the thread through to the knot or bead and then through one hole in the button and down through another hole in the button. Now poke the needle back down through another pencil mark on the circle. Unthread the needle and tie a fat knot or bead in the end of the thread. Now, cut a length of thread about three feet long and rethread the needle. Again, tie a fat knot or bead in the end. Poke the needle up through the remaining pencil mark on the circle. (Knots or beads should all be on the same side.) Pass the needle up through one of the remaining holes in the button and then down through the last hole. Unthread the needle and tie a loop in the end of the thread for hanging the mobile from the ceiling.

To hang the planets from the mobile frame, cut a long length of thread and thread the needle. Tie a knot or bead to the end. Draw the needle through the center of the galaxy. Now poke the needle through the appropriate orbit mark on the circle and through the corresponding cardboard cutout planet, thereby suspending the planet in the order in which it revolves around the Sun. Adjust the length of the thread so the planet hangs nicely, then cut the thread and tie a knot or bead in the end. Repeat this process for all of the planets. Make the planets hang at different levels, so they can turn freely without hitting each other.

Hang your solar system mobile from the ceiling. You can adjust the thread going through the button so that the circle is level.

Dream Catcher Mobile

Native American Dream Catchers symbolize traps that snare bad dreams and allow good dreams to filter through to the sleeper.

For this mobile, each child will need the following supplies:

- An embroidery hoop
- Beads with large holes
- Twine or thin wire
- A few feathers

1. Cut several feet of twine and tie one end to the hoop.
2. Have the child sting a few beads on the twine and wrap the twine around the other side of the hoop to anchor it.
3. Repeat this process with the same piece of twine until the child has created a pattern he or she likes.
4. Tie and knot the end of the twine around the hoop.
5. Cut off two or three short pieces of twine and tie them to the bottom of the hoop.
6. String some beads on each piece of twine and tie a feather on each end of the twine.
7. Hang the mobile–where else?–above the child's bed.

Resources

http://mips.as.arizona.edu/~stansber/Planet.html

This Website, entitled *Is Pluto a Planet,* defines and discusses planets, including Pluto's characteristics and place in the solar system.

www.mathcats.com/explore/virtual/mobile.html

This Website allows you to experiment with a virtual mobile on your computer screen.

How to Make Mobiles, (Search Press, 1997).

This book provides basic instructions about the construction and adjustment of mobiles.

Mobiles: Building and Experimenting with Balancing Toys, (Beech Tree Farm Publishers, 1993).

This Boston Children's Museum Activity Book offers simple activities to demonstrate various concepts of balance. The instructions are clear and designed to be followed by children in grades three to seven.

Alexander Calder and His Magical Mobiles, (Hudson Hills Press, 1981).

This book describes the life and career of artist Alexander Calder and includes illustrations of his most famous works and a guide to his sculptures in museums and public places.

Collages

A collage is an art form that is easy and fun for kids of all ages. The word comes from the French word colle, which means glued on. So the basic process is gluing different materials onto a base such as cardboard, poster board, fabric or even a sheet of paper. The result is a three-dimensional, textured piece of art.

Getting Started

Before you begin to create collages, you may want to visit a museum so that the kids can see various types of collages hanging on the museum walls. For the excursion to be meaningful, you should plan to visit only the collages in the museum. Therefore, you may prefer to visit on a free day rather than pay full admission to see only one type of art.

To begin to make collages at home, explain to the kids that a collage is a personal expression and, therefore, there are no rules. Each child can create a collage to represent who he or she is, what she likes or what she finds interesting to look at. Suggest themes to the kids–favorite singers or music groups, famous people, cars, horses–whatever you think might appeal to the kids. Then provide some old magazines, newspapers, wrapping paper, tissue paper, foil or even photographs (you may want to photocopy pictures that are valuable or are one-of-a-kind). Children's magazines as well as women's glossy magazines are especially good sources; both usually feature colorful photos of objects or scenes that are interesting to kids. Raid craft boxes for beads, feathers, string or fabric. Collect as many items as you can find and pile everything together on a table or on a drop cloth on the floor. If you have a protected spot outdoors, take everything there. Add scissors, glue and markers. Help each child select a base and then step back while they work.

Creating the Collage

If you are using magazines or newspapers, have the kids thumb through them, searching for interesting pictures that relate to their chosen theme. Tell the kids to cut out more pictures, letters or words than either of you think will be needed. This provides some flexibility in developing the design. Suggest they select what is important to the theme and what can be used as filler or left out. Have them cut, tear or trim the pieces going into the collage. Show them how to form the pieces into interesting shapes or how to cut pieces from different sources so that they fit together like a jigsaw puzzle. Do not throw away the scraps left over from the trimming. These scraps may later fill a hole in the collage background. Encourage them to lay out their final pieces on a table and arrange them in the most interesting way before gluing.

When the kids start gluing down the pieces, instruct them to spread the glue on thinly (to avoid saturating the piece and causing it to curl). Apply the piece to the base by pressing firmly on the center of the piece and then smoothing it out from the inside to the edges. This enables the pieces to overlap. A glue stick works well here because it easily allows the artist to peel off the piece and reapply it. Remember, you do not have to cover the entire base, nor do you have to glue each piece flat on the collage. Tucking crumbled paper or other items under flaps adds texture and relief to the collage. Point out to the kids that a unique characteristic of collages is the three-dimensional effect.

When the collages are finished, allow them to dry completely. This may take a few hours or even several days.

Selecting a Collage Theme

Although designing a collage is an individual expression, you can help your kids get started by suggesting some ideas.

Leaf Collage

This simple collage is a good way to introduce younger children to the art form. Take your kids for a walk and collect as many different leaves as you can find. Collect from trees, from bushes and from other plants as well.

Glue the leaves into a design on a cardboard base and then tuck in grasses or small twigs around the leaves. Another way to use the leaves is to have the kids use the glued-on leaves to represent body parts and then paint in the rest of the figure. As mentioned earlier, encourage the kids to strive for a three-dimensional form.

Alphabet Collage

Using old magazines and catalogs, have the kids search for each letter of the alphabet, cut it out and glue it onto a cardboard base. Then have the kids search again, this time for pictures of objects that begin with each letter of the alphabet. These pictures can be glued on in a design that is colorful and educational. For example, the objects do not have to appear next to their beginning letters; rather, scatter the objects about and then have the kids take turns matching letters to objects.

Nutrition Collage

Tell the kids to look through magazines and catalogs for foods that they should eat every day to grow and remain healthy. You can start by visiting *www.mypyramid.gov* to study the U.S. Department of Agriculture's (USDA) Food Pyramid. Before the kids start on their collages, talk about the pyramid and what kinds of foods belong to each food group. The kids can then design their collage around the Food Pyramid or around daily meals and snacks that include the foods as recommended by the Food Pyramid Website.

While you are on the subject, explore the USDA's site for other nutrition information geared toward children. For example, go to *www.mypyramid.gov/ kids/index.html* for activities and games that will teach your kids the basics of good nutrition and healthful living.

Vacation Collage

Creating a collage of snapshots and other mementos from a vacation is a good way to store your travel memories. Before you even leave on your trip, plan to collect mementos and keepsakes from your vacation to bring home for a collage.

Begin with color copies of your trip photos arranged in chronological order, by location or according to activity. Or your kids can decide to arrange the photos in any way that satisfies them. Intersperse other vacation keepsakes such as airline boarding passes, train tickets, event ticket stubs or matchbook covers from a memorable restaurant. Add three-dimensional items such as foreign coins, seashells or special leaves or rocks you found along the way. Mount everything on a board, frame it (as an option) and hang it as visible proof of the fun you and your family had on vacation.

Landscape Collages

Some kids like to recreate landscape scenes in their paintings and in their collages. Suggest to these children that they can create a neighborhood or a campsite, using fabric, rocks, toothpicks and other objects to denote a place or an atmosphere. The results can be amazing, particularly if the child uses all kinds of background filler and then add to the base of the collage her own constructed houses, schools or other buildings.

Shape and Color Experimental Collages

Rather than have the kids select a theme, urge them to make a collage using only one color but different shapes. Or confine the cutouts to one shape–say, a triangle–and have them construct a collage with items or pieces that are only triangular.

This is a good opportunity to talk about–and even assign the kids to do research on–Henri Matisse, a twentieth-century French painter who became famous in his later years for his colorful collages. Confined to a wheelchair because of illness, Matisse found it easier to create collages rather than paintings. Through his collages, he became famous for expressing relationships between color and shape.

Resources

You Can Make a Collage: A Very Simple How-To Book, (Klutz Press, 1998).

This book, aimed at preschoolers, offers step-by-step lessons from the author and collagist Eric Carle. The book includes sheets of multi-colored printed tissue paper, each of which is an original design by Carle.

www.mypyramid.gov

This is the United States Department of Agriculture (USDA) site that describes the Food Pyramid recommended for healthful eating and a healthy life-style.

Cardboard
Toys

A cardboard box is a parent's best friend. You have probably heard the age-old suggestion to send the toy back and let the kids play with the box it came in. In fact, the Strong Museum of Play in Rochester, New York, inducted the cardboard box into its Toy Hall of Fame in 2006, citing its "strength, light weight, easy availability and the many ways that a child's imagination could use boxes... for play."

Acquiring and Storing Cardboard

Cardboard's versatility and availability are two of its most important assets as you face a long summer of bored kids. Yet, you may think that acquiring and storing cardboard can be a problem. Acquiring cardboard does require diligence; you have to look for cardboard in everything you buy or receive. Cardboard is found in many everyday forms: the backs of writing tablets, stiffener boards from laundered shirts, food containers, shipping boxes, shoe boxes, paper towel tubes and toilet paper tubes. Save it all and stow it away for a rainy day. The only problem that baffles everyone is finding and storing large appliance boxes. You can obtain large boxes from appliance dealers, electronics stores and discount centers. Ask at the service desk and then be prepared to go to the shipping and receiving dock or waste center to pick up what you want. Storing large boxes may seem problematic, but that is easily solved if you break down boxes and other containers and then reassemble them using sturdy packing tape. Storing them after the kids have converted them into houses, ships, forts or robots is another dilemma. Be sure you have space for such creations before you suggest these activities to the kids.

Cardboard Projects

Here are some ideas for using the cardboard and the boxes you have accumulated. You may want to man the tape dispenser for big items, unless you have older kids who can manage this job.

Building Blocks

Save and rinse cardboard milk and juice containers. Cut off the pinched glued strip from the top and push out the twist-on dispenser lid. Have the kids gather about one cup of small rocks, dried beans or rice and pour these into the container, thus adding weight to the block. Fold the top down and tape it with duct tape. Show the kids how to cover the block with gray or red construction paper or adhesive paper to make stones or bricks. These can be stacked but do not attempt to walk on them.

Ping Pong Basketball

This project requires an empty oatmeal box and a small plastic drinking cup. Let the kids cover the oatmeal box with construction paper and decorate it. Make a basketball basket by cutting the bottom from the drinking cup–you may want to supervise this since the plastic cup can acquire sharp edges when cut. Tape the cup to the side of the oatmeal box.

Set a time limit at the beginning of each basketball game. To play, the kids take turns trying to bounce a ping pong ball into the paper cup basket. Each basket is worth two points. When the time runs out, the player with the most points is the winner.

Paper Dolls

This is a project that preschool-age kids enjoy doing. Trace outlines of human figures from a magazine or coloring book or have the kids draw a silhouette of their dolls. Cut these out and trace around them on some poster board or cardboard. Cut out the cardboard figures and let the kids color in a face, fingers and other body parts. Show them how to glue on yarn or cotton balls for hair. Finally, glue on small pieces of Velcro™ at the neck, wrists, waist and ankles.

Using fabric scraps, fashion clothing to fit each doll. Ask your kids for suggestions about the clothing and encourage them to glue on small buttons or trim. Glue small pieces of Velcro on the back of the doll clothes to match the Velcro on the doll silhouettes. Help your kids make several changes of clothing so that they can make up stories and dress their dolls to match the action.

Cardboard Guitar

Cardboard boxes lend themselves to becoming musical instruments. Show your kids how to make a guitar by cutting a four-inch diameter hole in the top of a shoe box or a corrugated shipping box. Be sure to use a box that your child can hold comfortably. Let the kids decorate their guitars by painting them or gluing on designs. Stretch four or more rubber bands around the box to cross the opening in the top. Explain that thin, tight rubber bands create high-pitched sounds while thick, looser rubber bands make lower-pitched sounds.

Box Village

Using small boxes of different sizes and shapes to create a toy village challenges your children's imagination and math skills. Selecting box sizes and laying out a town teaches proportion and scale.

To make buildings, wrap small boxes in construction paper and draw the features of buildings on them. You or an older child can cut out windows or doors. Use toilet paper tubes for chimneys and cotton balls for smoke coming from the chimneys. The kids can also paint decorations (stair steps, window boxes or shutters) on the buildings. If your kids want an urban atmosphere, have them use oatmeal boxes for skyscrapers or high rises. For a country scene, the oatmeal boxes can become grain silos.

To make trees, use a toilet paper tube or a paper towel tube (depending on the proportion of surrounding buildings) for the tree trunks. Draw or paint green leaf canopies on the cardboard and then cut them out and tape them to the trunks.

To complete the town, you can lay out the streets and other landmarks using tape. See the chapter on Indoor Games with Tape for ideas.

Cardboard Dollhouse

This project requires one large corrugated cardboard box, different-sized small boxes, fabric scraps, craft scraps and markers. The final touch, of course, is a doll family.

Place the large cardboard box on a table or shelf for easy reach. A good choice is a box with cardboard inserts to hold glass bottles–the criss-crossed inserts can be fashioned into floors or levels. Paint or decorate the house and cut out some windows and/or doors.

If you have a carpet remnant, help the kids install wall-to-wall carpeting. Or they can make rugs from fabric scraps. Cut out pictures from magazines or use stickers to decorate the walls. Wrap small boxes (use empty food boxes from products such as pudding, gelatin or rice) to create furniture. Wooden blocks can also become furniture or appliances. Pudding cups become plumbing fixtures, thimbles become waste baskets, checkbook boxes become beds. Encourage the kids to look around your own home for dollhouse furnishings.

The Big Box Home

Obtain a large appliance box (a refrigerator box is good) and tell the kids to make a house. They can paint the interior and exterior (do not forget to paint or tape artificial flowers and shrubs on the outside walls) and mark off windows and doors. Suggest a two-piece Dutch door. Using a box cutter or utility knife, you or another adult can cut out windows, doors, skylights or pet exits. Working with what you can gather around the house, install window boxes, curtains, throw rugs, furniture and household equipment. Help your kids use smaller cardboard boxes to create furniture, even suggesting that they can take turns being the entertainment behind the cut-out TV screen. If the house is large enough, they can even pull in their sleeping bags for sleepovers.

If you have enough space—a large basement or playroom, for example—you can even tape several large boxes together to create a multi-room home. This will accommodate several children at once and will most probably become a neighborhood attraction.

No matter what size house you build, however, be sure that you have enough space to leave it set up for a long period of time. This is an activity that the kids will enjoy coming back to all summer.

Resources

www.strongmuseum.org

This is the official Website of the Strong National Museum of Play in Rochester, New York. You can explore the site for games to play, and if you visit *www.strongmuseum.org/kids/tangrams.html,* you will find an ancient Chinese game called tangrams that you can download, cut and glue the parts to cardboard and play with your kids.

The Most Incredible Cardboard Toys in the Whole Wide World,
(Lark Books, 1999).

This book contains instructions to make 17 well-designed toys, each inspired by a different country and accompanied by an educational story.

Beach
Games

If you are fortunate enough to live near a river, lake or ocean, you can make beach days part of your summer schedule. If you do not live near a body of water, then you can usually adapt beach games to the swimming pool or sometimes a backyard wading pool.

The first consideration around water is safety. The adult-to-child ratio should always be high, particularly if you have young children or children who cannot swim. In addition, the swimmer- to-nonswimmer ratio should be high; a nonswimming adult supervising one or more children is not necessarily a safe practice.

The children, too, must understand the importance of safety around water and the seriousness of obeying instructions from lifeguards or adults. You do not want to frighten your kids, but they need to know how to be safe around water. You should revisit safety rules before each day at the beach.

Water games are fun and allow you to keep an eye on your kids while you participate. If you are concerned that the games will be lopsided because of differing ages and skill levels, you can equalize the playing field by having adults or strong swimmers swim with one arm; also, you can boost a kid's swimming speed by having him or her wear flippers.

Beach games, too, require supervision. There is always the safety issue if the game or participants straggle out into the water. But you also need to guard against sunburn and heat stroke if you are out in the sun all day. Be sure to use an appropriate sunscreen on your kids, reapplying it at intervals as they wash it off in the water or as they sweat during the day.

Beach Activities

You and the kids may want to split your time at the beach between water games and beach activities. After all, the point of playing near a body of water is to take advantage of the opportunity of going in the water to cool off whenever the sun gets too hot. Here are a few games and activities that you and the kids can enjoy in the water and on the beach.

Toy Race

Find a place in the water away from other beach visitors and set up some racing boundaries in the water. The object of the race is to swim while pushing a rubber ducky or toy–by nudging it with your nose or pushing it with your chin–from the starting line to the finish line. The first person to reach the finish line is the winner. If you do not have floating toys, you and the kids can make some by dropping some pebbles or sand into empty plastic soft drink bottles and capping them. The pebbles help stabilize the bottles when they are put into water.

Water Relay Races

Using the race boundaries you have already set up, form teams of swimmers by counting off or teaming kids (and adults) by categories. For example, you can team dads versus moms, families versus families or boys versus girls. It is up to the competitors how they want to form teams. The race requires one member of each team to swim one lap from the starting line to the finish line while performing an activity. For instance, the boys can swim while pushing a beach ball ahead of themselves with their nose, and the girls can do the backstroke while singing the ABC song. When a team member finishes a lap, the next person on the team does her lap while performing the assigned activity until everyone on the team has had a turn. The first team to finish is the winner.

Magnetic Moms

This is a great game for large family reunions that are held at the beach. All the kids and their mothers wade into the water at the same time. The mothers close their eyes and count to 10 in unison. The kids, meanwhile, scatter out into the shallow areas of the water in groups of siblings. When the mothers reach the number 10, they call out to their children who begin to call back by yelling out–mom–individually. With their eyes closed, the mothers begin to search for their children by listening to the children's voices. The first mother to reach her group of children wins.

This is a good game to signal the end of the day. The mothers gather up their kids in the water and get ready to go home.

Beach Bowling

Make bowling pins by filling a tall plastic cup or a small bucket with wet sand, then turning it over and lifting off the cup. Repeat this action 10 times in order to create 10 bowling pins, lining them up in the traditional bowling triangle with one in front, two in the second row, three in the third row and four in the last row. Draw a line in the sand about six-to-eight feet away from the pins. Each player stands behind the line and rolls a softball or a soccer ball toward the pins. After each player rolls twice, count how many pins have been hit and keep score in the sand. Replace the pins so that the next player can roll. The person with the highest score at the end of the game is the winner.

Darts in the Sand

Draw a large circle in the sand, inscribing six concentric circles inside with a twig. Assign each interior circle a point value. Have the kids gather enough markers from the beach so that each player has three similar ones. Each child takes a turn tossing a marker at the dartboard, keeping score in the sand. The person with the highest score at the end of the game is the winner.

Nekki—Sand Horseshoes

This game is similar to the game of horseshoes only without the horseshoes. Originating in Japan, the object of the game is to knock down a target stick called a nekki by throwing smaller sticks at it.

Find one sturdy target stick and a playing stick for each player, all about one-foot long. Gather some smaller, thinner sticks to mark the throwing lines. Push the target stick down into the sand so that it is upright and firmly anchored. Mark off the throwing area from the target stick to the starting line with the smaller sticks. If the kids are of different ages and skill levels, set up two or more starting lines to accommodate different abilities. Each child takes a turn throwing a stick at the nekki. The winner is the first person to knock down the target stick. This game does require some supervision from an adult or an older child to ensure that no one crosses into the throwing area.

Sand Sculptures

A visit to the beach is not complete without a sand castle event. You can turn it into a competition or encourage your kids to create sand sculptures around which they can develop an imaginary game or story.

The typical sand castle is always fun. Using plastic cups and sand buckets, the kids can create a fairy tale castle complete with turrets, moats and fortified walls. If they want to move beyond this into different or larger sand sculptures, suggest that the kids search the beach area for sticks, shells, vegetation or rocks and devise a scene using these finds.

For example, the kids could build a vehicle. Mound the sand into a pile large enough to hold one or two seated children when hollowed out. Hollow out the interior of the mound and shape seats and a dashboard. On the outside, add wet sand to the sides and mold fenders and wheels. Add some large rocks for headlights and taillights. Pretend that the car is an open convertible or a flatbed truck. Insert a stick at the side of the vehicle where the windshield would be and hang a seaweed flag. Carve logos on the hood, create a hood ornament from sticks and rocks and design wheel covers from shells. Let the kids' imaginations run free. They may become so enthusiastic that they build a fleet of vehicles for different uses.

Resources

Swimming and Aquatic Safety Handbook

> Available from your local Red Cross, this handbook offers detailed information on swimming safety.

www.escapemaker.com/outdoors/raftingandtubing.html

> This Website lists different locations where you and your family can go to participate in rafting and tubing. The locations are categorized by states, and there is an events calendar to help you plan your outings.

www.kidsturncentral.com/links/beachsports.htm

> This Website offers online beach games for those days when the weather prevents you from going to the beach.

www.houghtonmifflinbooks.com/peterson/seashore.cfm

> This Website lists titles of Peterson Field Guides to seashores, shells and coral reefs. For parents, the series entitled *First Guide* is especially helpful when working with young children.

24

Car
Games

Are we there yet? What parent has not cringed when hearing these words uttered by a child before even leaving the outskirts of the neighborhood? The only other question that provokes an equally deep sigh from a traveling parent is, How much farther?

You may be able to avoid these questions with a little planning. Here are a few suggestions:

Pack a Goodie Bag For Each Child

Try to include toys and craft materials appropriate to each child's age. Younger children like crayons, drawing paper, small individual games, decks of cards, puzzles, stickers and books. Older kids appreciate books, decks of cards, notebooks, CDs and maps. You can also include snacks, particularly healthy food and water bottles. Avoid sugar, since there is no sense in creating a sugar energy high when everyone has to sit in the car for long periods of time.

Allow For Frequent Stops

This allows everyone, especially kids, to stretch, walk or run around. Kids are seldom content to sit still for long periods of time, so stop often to give them a chance to run off some bottled-up energy.

Change Car Seats Occasionally

If the kids start to bicker or fight, it may be time to switch seating arrangements. Use pillows to separate those kids who cannot avoid tickling, pinching or otherwise tormenting their seatmates.

Pack Books on Tape For the Entire Family to Enjoy

Check your local library or rental video store for these items.

Pass Out the Headphones if Nothing Else Works

If nothing else works, sometimes the only way to restore peace and quiet among the kids is to allow one or all of them to put on headphones and listen to a favorite CD. Some families even carry portable DVD players that work on the car's cigarette lighter. Although your goal is to discourage long periods of time in front of a screen, using electronic entertainment devices may be necessary on a long road trip.

Travel at Night

If night driving is difficult for you, try it in the late afternoon or in the very early morning when the kids can sleep.

Play Games

This is where planning comes into play. Be prepared to suggest or provide games to help while away the hours in the car.

Provide each child with a three-ring binder that can also serve as a playing board, a writing board and a drawing board. Include lots of different kinds of notebook paper–lined, plain and graph. Drop pens, pencils, markers and crayons into a self-closing plastic bag or a manila envelope into which you punch three holes so that it can be carried in the notebook. Add a three-hole punched empty plastic bag to hold mementos and brochures. Clamp two or three binder clips onto the notebook cover. Glue some felt to the back of it so that there is a nonskid surface on which to play cards or work puzzles.

This notebook is so convenient that you may want to make one for yourself.

Here are some games that may keep your kids busy and interested on those long car rides.

Counting Cows

The old standby, counting cows, sheep, horses, barns or whatever strikes anyone's fancy, is always worth a try.

There are several ways to play, depending on the age and abilities of the children. The kids can compete as individuals or as teams. If you divide them into teams, tell one team to count the designated object, for example, cows, from one side of the car and tell the other team to count cows from the other side of the car. Assign a point value to each item the teams are counting; for example, a cow is worth one point, a black sheep is worth two points, a red barn is worth 10 points and a green house is worth 50 points. The team with the most points wins. Have the kids devise their own scoring system before they start. One of the pluses of this game is the opportunity to distract the other team so that their players miss cows on their side of the road.

Progressive Drawing

Take a sheet of paper and ask the kids to take turns drawing a composite picture. You can start by sketching something you see in the passing scenery. Then each person adds to the picture, again drawing an item or building they see outside. When the page is filled, you should have a cohesive drawing of the scenery.

Progressive Storytelling

Like progressive drawing, this game is a method of developing a cohesive story with each participant adding a sentence at a time. You may want to start the first sentence and then ask the kids to take turns adding one sentence at a time. This may be easier for younger children who have not yet mastered drawing or writing techniques. Older children can write down the story as it unfolds.

Alphabet Story

Ask the kids to plan a trip (other than the one you are taking) and itemize what they will pack. The first player announces, I am going to China, and I am going to pack (an object that begins with the letter A). The second player continues with an object that begins with the letter B and on throughout the alphabet. The objects do not have to be logical—someone could pack a dolphin, for example. In fact, the sillier the better.

Secret Codes

Ask your kids to use road maps or the road atlas to find symbols that they can assign to letters of the alphabet. Be sure each child has a sheet of symbols written next to each letter. Once that is completed, the kids can write notes in code to each other and maybe even construct short stories that way. Older children can help younger children, or you can devise a simple code system for children who are just beginning to read.

Concentration

Glue or tape a piece of felt on the back of one of the children's notebooks or to a clipboard before you leave home. Tuck into one of the empty plastic bags some small squares (one-inch by one-inch) of felt that are all the same color but that are a contrasting color to the glued felt. Ask each child to draw symbols or letters on the felt squares with a marker. There should be at least one pair of squares for each symbol. Lay out the squares face down on the clipboard in even rows. Select the first player by either counting off or tossing a die. Player #1 turns over two squares and if they do not match turns them back face down. Player #2 then turns over two squares, again looking for a match. As the game progresses, children will begin to remember the location of each turned down symbol or letter. When a child matches two squares, he or she picks up the squares and wins another turn until turning up a mismatch. The child with the most pairs at the end of the game wins.

Map Games

Provide each child with a road map. Ask the kids to:

- Plot the route to your destination;
- plot a different way home;
- figure out the fastest route as opposed to the most scenic route to a destination;
- trace roads to create a picture of an animal, person or object; or
- find names of cities whose names begin with a certain letter.

Traveling Puppets

Take along some brown paper lunch bags or old socks to create puppets as you travel. Have the kids use markers or crayons to add features and decorations to their puppets. They can then devise puppet scenarios by placing their hands inside the bottom of the bag or sock and creating a puppet mouth from the folded-over part of the bag or the toe of the sock. The puppets can be easily folded up and tucked away after the show.

Postcards

Carry some blank postcards and stamps to make postcards to mail to friends back home. And when you stop for a meal or to rest, look for postcards of the region you are visiting. Once back in the car, the kids can create their own postcard scenes on one side of the blank postcards and write notes to friends on the other side. Or they can jot down notes to friends on the purchased cards. Mail them at the next rest stop.

A Math Problem

Challenge your kids to answer their own question, How much farther? Explain that the answer is the solution to the formula, distance equals rate multiplied by time $(D=R \times T)$.

Start with simple questions. If you are driving at 50 miles per hour, how many hours will it take to travel 150 miles? Or if you are driving at 40 miles per hour, how many miles can you travel in 5 hours? Try some harder questions: If your destination is 130 miles away (according to a roadside sign), how long will it take to get there if you are driving at 45 miles per hour?

Ask the kids to recalculate every time they see another roadside mileage sign. They can also figure in the time you spend at stops or meals and the time it takes to maneuver through city traffic or a speed zone. Some of these calculations will be too difficult for younger children, but the older ones will enjoy the challenge posed by changing traffic conditions.

Resources

Smart Play/Smart Toys, (Educational Insights, 2004).
www.drtoy.com

> This book and Website recommend educational toys and products to use with children while traveling. The author describes each recommendation and gives its advantages and disadvantages as well as its suitability for various age levels.

www.autoclubgroup.com

> This is the Website of AAA, and it offers information about traveling with children. Look for travel tips and articles, including articles about traveling with tots. Also, the organization provides Online TourBooks® and AAA Internet TripTik®/Traveler to help you plan your trips. Best of all, AAA has an extensive map selection that you can use for some of your car games.

25

Keeping a Journal of
Summer Fun

Creating and maintaining a journal of summer activities is a wonderful way to document what you and the kids did all summer. The journal can be simple, fancy or both, depending on the ages and personalities of the kids. When you suggest the idea, ask the kids how they want to proceed. Do they want to develop the journal as a group or does each one want to contribute his or her own pages? How do the kids want to focus the journal–around individual activities or chronological events? Will there be an overall theme? Finally, who takes the photos and who writes the captions?

Supplies

Once you have decided on a basic plan, you can get started. No matter how you create the journal, you will need some supplies:

Album

The simplest album is a loose-leaf notebook that can accommodate as many pages as you want to include and that offers the flexibility to put the pages where you want them to go. The kids can decorate the album cover with paper and then cut out letters or words from magazines to create the title and other information for the cover. Another decorating idea is to use rub-on lettering and letter stickers. The kids can also glue fabric scraps or paint drawings onto the cover. When they are finished, show them how to coat the entire album surface with transparent self-adhesive paper to keep it clean and tatter-free.

Paper or Filler

You can use plain white paper, but it will probably not have enough body to hold photos and art projects. Therefore, you might want to look for heavier paper (try journaling or scrapbooking sections of craft stores). Offer the kids some variety–smooth, textured, colored or white. And if the album is to become a permanent keepsake, look for acid-free paper that will not yellow or deteriorate. If you are using a loose-leaf binder, you may need to purchase a hole punch or shop for paper with drilled holes.

Glue or Adhesives

You can provide the usual white glue, but glue sticks may be a better choice here. As with collages and other art forms, a glue stick allows the kids to peel off and reposition the pieces—an important consideration when you are trying to plan and arrange a balanced page containing many elements. Plus a glue stick is less messy, an advantage if your kids are young. If you do not want to use glue, double-sided adhesive tape is a good substitute, although it does not peel off as readily.

Scissors, Markers, Pens and Rulers

Blunt-tipped safety scissors may not be adequate for these activities, particularly if you are trying to trim photos or other stiff materials. Provide safety scissors but also be ready to help younger kids use sharp scissors to work on the project. A ruler should be flat and easy to read.

Photos and Mementos

Gather together all the photos and mementos of your summer projects and activities. If your photos were taken with a digital camera or a cell phone, print out the pictures so that you are working with hard copy.

Getting Started

If you and the kids want to create an album to showcase all of your summer activities, then you should make plans at the beginning of the summer. If, however, you do not think about making an album until the summer is half over, you can still take on the project at any point. No matter when you start, if you want to feature photos in the album, then you should be certain that everyone who is old enough has access to a camera. Older kids may own and use a cell phone with a camera or they can use a digital camera. Younger kids, however, can usually learn how to take pictures with a disposable camera. Show the children how to turn on the camera and focus on the subject. Explain how to frame their view and examine what they see in the viewfinder before they snap the picture. Most kids four years and older can learn how to use a camera. Look for coupons for disposable cameras and two-for-one specials. Each child can have a camera or they can share one.

In addition to photos, cultivate the habit of collecting mementos and keepsakes of the places you visit—interesting leaves, wild flowers or ticket stubs. They can go into the album along with the photos. The kids' artwork or projects can be highlighted in the album as well; if they are too large, take a photo of the art pieces. The point is that you should always be on the lookout for items to include in the album so that you have a personal history of what the family did all summer.

After assembling all the photos and other pieces, you can begin to create the album. If the kids want it to be chronological, then gather together all the pieces for a day or a period of time. The first step is to crop the photos, that is, cut out the parts of the photo you want to show. You may want to make copies so that you do not ruin the originals. You can cut the photos into traditional squares or rectangles, or you can trim them into shapes for variety. You can also mat the photos, that is, place a colored mat (larger than the photo) on the page behind each picture to highlight it. Most very young kids have no patience for matting, but older kids like the finished look.

Have the kids arrange the photos and mementos on the page until they achieve a look they like. Then, before gluing down the pieces, ask the kids to write a caption or a story about the picture or object on a separate sheet of paper. This is called journaling, and it is an important part of finishing a family album. Younger children may need to dictate their story to you or to an older child. When the kids finish their journaling, show them how to arrange the photos so that enough space is left to accommodate the written details. Then they can mount the mats, photos and mementos, they can copy the journaling and they can add decorations to the page.

Tips for Adding Extras

Some situations involve extra planning:

- If your kids want to include small, flat art objects or creations, create a pocket page by gluing or taping half of a page to the bottom of a full-sized page. If the art does not fit this pocket, enclose it in a plastic sleeve protector into which you punch holes so that it can go in the binder.
- If a piece of art is too large to fit into the album, photocopy it at a reduced size. You can have the child write the journal portion on the original art itself and then reduce the entire piece to fit the album or you can include the journal piece after the page has been reduced and photocopied.
- If members of your family like to add comments about their version of the event described on each page, be sure to leave some space somewhere on the page for this journaling. And do not forget to remind the creator of each page to sign her name on the sheet.

The Main Goal

Your primary goal for this activity is to ensure that your kids have fun while reliving an enjoyable occasion. No matter how much you strive for a consistent look to the album, remember that allowing the kids to exercise their own creativity is more important. They can decide to work together or to make individual contributions to the album, but whatever the result, you should step back and let them have fun documenting their own memories.

Resources

All About Me: A Keepsake Journal for Kids, (Rising Moon Books, 2004).

This book, geared toward kids, gives tips on constructing and maintaining a personal journal.

All Kids Scrapbook: The Growing Up Years, (Memory Makers Books, 2005).

This book provides suggestions on how to take photos and use them in a scrapbook or album. In addition, it offers fresh ideas for page layout.

www.activityvillage.co.uk/scrapbook%20paper.htm

This Website offers free scrapbook paper designs for scrapbooks and crafts.

http://library.thinkquest.org/J001156/makingbooks/sc_clothcovered.htm

This Website gives instructions, along with illustrations, for creating your own hardcover bookbinding.

www.bodegabooks.com

This Website highlights the book *Now and Then,* which shows children a fun and easy way to make a scrapbook of their mementos and memories. There is an easy fill-in format for documenting their growing-up years and free printable pages you can download to get started.

26

Scavenger Hunt

A scavenger hunt is one of the most versatile activities you can plan. You can hold it indoors or outdoors, you can play it as team members or as individuals, you can use a list of instructions or follow a map, you can have a theme or go without one and you can offer prizes to the victor or allow the win itself to be ample reward.

Granted, a good scavenger hunt requires planning. But think about the advantages of the hunt. Not only is it fun, but a hunt encourages cooperating as a group, solving problems, following directions and reasoning. What better way for kids to acquire these skills than to learn to use them in the process of reaching a goal?

You can plan one of two types of scavenger hunts: a treasure hunt or a scavenger hunt. Kids like either kind, and you will find that they develop the same learning skills in either one.

Treasure Hunts

For a simple treasure hunt, you will need to collect treasure pieces, such as plastic coins, play money, toy jewelry or small toys. You can stock up at party stores without spending too much money. Or you can find treasures around the house to put in the chest, such as snack packages, fruit or coins. Create a treasure chest by locating a small cardboard box or a carton that the kids can decorate. After they have finished decorating it, it is your turn to fill the box and hide it. Select a hiding place either inside or outdoors in the yard. You may want to set some boundaries on the search area, such as within the backyard or only on the first floor of the house.

Your next step is to prepare clues for finding the treasure. You can write out clues or draw pictures if your kids do not yet read. Give each kid or team of kids the clues–usually in sequential order–and send them off on the hunt. Or you can hide all but the first clue and ask the children to find the clues as the first step toward locating the treasure chest. For example, clue #1 may direct the participants to walk 20 paces to the oak tree where they will find clue #2, which will, in turn, steer the kids to the next clue and so on.

Clues for a Treasure Hunt

The key to a great treasure hunt is the set of clues. Creating the clues allows you to use your ingenuity and imagination, and interpreting the clues is often the most fun for the kids. For example, you can write, draw or photograph clues and then cut them up into several pieces that the hunters have to reconstruct (printouts of digital photos work best). You can put the pieces in an envelope along with a small tape dispenser to hold the clue together. Each clue leads to the next one, which is also cut into pieces of a puzzle. At the end of a predetermined number of clues (which you inform the kids about), the kids should discover the treasure and open it together.

Another variation is to place pieces of clues inside plastic eggs or small boxes. The children search the area to find as many eggs as possible and then bring them back to the starting point. There, working as a team, the kids will reconstruct the puzzle and tape it together. On the back of the puzzle is a final clue, directing the players toward the treasure. You can use a series of pictures or you can phrase the clue as a poem, a song or a riddle. Together the kids work out the meaning and run to uncover the treasure's hiding place.

You can also create straightforward clues but written (or printed) backwards so that the players have to find a mirror to read them. Or, depending on the age and maturity of the kids, you can use the clues to send children throughout the house into the dark basement or garage, providing flashlights to illuminate the way. Hide clues under objects, shelves or furniture that have been draped in sheets to look spooky. This version is also an interesting way to conduct a scavenger hunt in which the kids look for objects to scavenge rather than clues to follow.

Treasure Chest

A cardboard carton makes a fine treasure chest, but if you want to be a little more inventive, try making a papier-mâché treasure box (see the chapter on papier-mâché). You can create a capsule or round rock structure by smoothing papier-mâché over an inflated balloon into which you have inserted small toys and other treasures. Once the papier-mâché coating has dried, pop the balloon, and you will have a different kind of treasure chest. You can even have the kids help you construct the treasure chest ahead of time.

Scavenger Hunts

The simplest scavenger hunt can be impromptu. Give the kids a list of objects (a doll with a blue dress, a toy truck or a musical instrument) to look for in your house or yard. Send them off as individual hunters or as teams. Whoever returns first with all of the items on the list is the winner.

Give each child a brown bag to hold his or her scavenged items. If the kids are working as teams, provide each team with an identifying tag; for example, the teams can wear bandannas, hats, paper badges or ribbons of different colors to differentiate one team from the others. Leave it up to the teams to decide if they want to work as a group or divide up the items on the list to finish sooner.

Nature Hunt

An even easier scavenger hunt is the nature hunt for which you give the kids a brown bag and a list–or even dictate a list–of nature items they can find in the yard or park. Include specific kinds of leaves, nuts, seeds, wild flowers, weeds, rocks, twigs or pine cones. Add in something red, something yellow and something blue. The first team to return with all of the items is the winner.

Neighborhood Scavenging

A more ambitious activity is the neighborhood scavenger hunt in which you arrange to have the kids ask neighbors to help them meet the requirements on the list. You should try this only if you have a friendly tight-knit neighborhood– or apartment building– whose inhabitants know the kids and are willing to cooperate. Be sure to send a request to your neighbors, describing the game and asking them to participate. If someone does not want to be disturbed, then be sure to tell the kids to skip that home.

Limit the kids to two or three items per house and be clear that the items are to be disposable. Your list should, therefore, include only objects that are of little value to the original owners. You can set a point value on each type of item to enable the kids to compete for the most points. For instance, a button, empty toilet paper roll, canceled stamp or a rubber band could be worth one point. Rarer items, such as a holiday paper plate, an empty fruit cocktail can or a blue ribbon, can be worth two points. Use your imagination to set up a point system that presents a challenge to the players. Naturally, the team with the most points is the winner.

A variation of this type of hunt is to collect objects of increasing size. For example, give each team a screw or bolt and an assigned territory in the neighborhood. The kids go to each house in their territory and ask if the residents have anything bigger than a screw to trade. The teams continue to trade up in size at different homes until they cannot get anything larger or until the allotted time is up. The winner is the team with the largest item.

Museum or Zoo Scavenger Hunt

Contact a local museum or zoo to obtain maps of the facility. Map out a tour of the museum or zoo that directs the kids through the entire facility. The items to be scavenged (or located and identified) along the way are specific pieces of art or displays in each room of the museum or certain animals in each section of the zoo. Provide the kids with a checklist of the items to be found and have each child check off each finding by writing down one characteristic of the display or animal. By the end of the tour, your list should direct the kids to a lunchroom or park area where you can meet to talk about the hunt. The prize is lunch at the museum or zoo.

Resources

www.education-world.com/a_curr/curr113.shtml

This Website features online scavenger hunting to teach kids how to use resources on the Internet.

http://k-6educators.about.com/library/howto/htscav.htm

This Website shows parents and teachers how to make online scavenger hunts to help kids learn Web browsing and research skills.

A Train Trip

An old-fashioned train ride can be an exciting adventure for kids. Younger children enjoy the ride itself, especially if they have never ridden on a train. Older kids, on the other hand, may enjoy the ride more if they learn ahead of time about the history of the railroads and their impact on transportation. In this age of space exploration, air flight and instantaneous communications through the Internet, many kids view trains and railroads as extinct phenomena from the distant past. But reading about the history of railroads in North America can be fascinating, and a planned train excursion is a good opportunity to learn about that period in history. The rail industry was an early step in expanding horizons beyond your hometown to–eventually–virtual space.

Short Train Excursions

If you live in an urban area where ground-level trains and elevated trains (ELs) are a part of a public transportation system, you can easily plan a train trip. If you are unfamiliar with the public transit system, check the phone book for their customer service number or visit their Website. Most sites provide routes, maps, schedules, fares and points of interest along the way. This is also an opportunity to enhance your trip by selecting an interesting destination to visit on the train route.

When you plan the excursion, print out the map of the route you have chosen or obtain a map that incorporates transit routes of the area. This is a good time to teach the kids how to read maps and to familiarize them with their hometown. If you have a destination in mind, ask the kids to plan the most logical way to get there. Give them a highlighting marker to draw the route on the map.

Planning your trip is essential in order to avoid problems. First, arrange to take the trip during non-rush hours. The trains will not be as crowded, and each kid may be able to snag a window seat. Bear in mind that there may be fewer trains scheduled during non-rush hours, so it may take you a little longer to get to your destination. Second, you will probably need exact change for the fare. Some systems require that you buy a train pass before you board, so allow time to do so for everyone. The transit Website should list fares. In some places, infants and toddlers can ride free or pay only half fare. Others base the child's fare on age or height. Be certain you are clear about the regulations in your area because you will have to have exact change for all the fares before boarding the train. And do check the availability of all-day passes so that you can get on and off whenever you want without paying a new fare.

If your kids are young, you may want to pack a small bag consisting of a travel game, a small pad for taking notes, a camera, snacks, extra clothes and towelettes. Older kids may bring along their own cameras and CD players with earphones—many transit systems prohibit radios and CD players that are not accompanied by earphones. You may be happy to have these distractions to occupy the kids but encourage them to look out at the scenery. If each kid has a map of the route, he or she can follow your progress and learn about your town in the process.

As a safety precaution print your cell phone number on business-sized cards and hand one ot each child. In the event a child gets separated from the group, they can call you and tell you where they are.

After you have visited your selected destination—such as a museum, a restaurant, a store or, best of all, a railroad museum—revisit your maps and select your route home. Do not forget to watch the clock during your visit so that you can travel home before evening rush hour begins. And do not forget that you will need exact change once again for the fares home, unless of course you have bought an all-day pass.

Once you have returned home, urge the kids to jot down what they found memorable about the excursion so that they can more accurately recall the day when they mount their photos into a memory album. Also, try to get a comment about the trip from each child so that you know how to plan the next one.

Longer Train Excursions

The best resource for planning longer train trips is Amtrak's Website at *www.amtrak.com.* Plan to spend some time visiting this site. You can learn about excursion trains in different regions, and you can find out what amenities Amtrak offers.

Amenities

Amenities are important if you are traveling with kids. For example, Amtrak has a no-smoking policy on its trains and in most of its stations. The company also offers a Quiet Car^{SM} service on many of its trains to provide a quiet atmosphere for those who want to work or rest without noise or distraction. Devices that make noise–such as cell phones, games or CD players without headphones as well as laptop computers with audible features–are banned from use in the Quiet Car. While your kids may not be able to meet these standards, a sleeping child may be able to finish a nap there.

You can also rent a portable digital entertainment device preloaded with movies, music videos, destination information and route guides if you think the kids need entertainment on the trip. Naturally, you want to encourage them to watch the scenery, but for those journeys that run into evening hours, the entertainment center may be helpful.

Look into the food facilities on each train. Some offer a full dining car while others provide a snack bar or cold food facility. You will probably want to pack a travel bag with snacks and drinks, but you and the kids may find a trip to the snack bar a treat.

When you do pack your carry-on bag, include a pair of binoculars, notepads, a couple of books, maps and a camera. If your train excursion ends at a destination or if you will be making stops at points of interest during the trip, be sure your bag is easily portable while you are walking around. Toting an overflowing bag on a sightseeing walk while herding three or four children, each with a blanket, a pillow and a stuffed toy, can become wearing.

Fares

Investigate fares for kids. A child's fare is often lower, even as much as 50 percent lower, than the adult price. Be sure to check the rules for infants riding free–do the rules entitle the baby to a seat or must he sit on an adult's lap? Look, too, for special deals–two-for-one sales, holiday fares and limited-time deals. Do not confine your search only to kids' fares; see if you, too, can get a cheaper ticket.

Destinations

Explore the Internet for interesting destinations. The Capitol Corridor *(www.capitolcorridor.org)* offers a route through points of interest in northern California. You can choose which segment of the route you want to travel. In addition, there is a one-day excursion train from New York City to Washington DC *(www.allnewyorktours.com)* that visits some important sightseeing spots in the nation's capital. Also, another Amtrak resource, *www.amtrakvacations.com,* provides lists of train excursions in the East (including Baltimore, Boston, Miami and Toronto, among others), the Midwest (Chicago, Dallas, Memphis, Minneapolis and St. Louis) and the West (Grand Canyon, Las Vegas, Los Angeles, San Francisco and Vancouver).

How about New England? Visit *www.visitnewengland.com* to learn about short scenic round-trips through New England on restored locomotives and coaches. Many of the excursions are tied to an historic railroad museum where activities that are geared toward children are featured. Other similar excursion plans are available in other geographic regions as well where historic sites and rail museums are the highlights of the trip *(http://familyfun.go.com/family-travel/places/feature/famf0800trains/)*.

Resources

www.vacationsbyrail.com

This Website lists train vacations on Amtrak, including escorted tours and tours by region. You can also participate in online travel seminars.

www.trainweb.com/travel

The Website also lists train vacations and includes links to travel agents, travelogues and travel itineraries.

www.railkids.com

This Website provides games and jokes about trains and train travel that are geared toward kids.

www.railserve.com/Tourist/North_America/

This Website has information about tourist railroads and museums in North America. The information is categorized by region including Central, Eastern (Eastern and Atlantic), Mountain and Pacific.

www.20thcentury.org

This is the official Website of the 20th Century Railroad Club. Named after the 20th Century Limited express passenger train operated by the New York Central Railroad from 1902 to 1967 between New York City and Chicago, the club arranges 1- to 4-day train excursions and tours, vacation trips and chartered tours. Most tours are open to the public.

28

Excursions:
Trip to the Museum

A trip to a museum–either a familiar one or a new one–is a fun outing for most children. To ensure that it is fun for everyone, start with a few basic guidelines. First, try to avoid the busiest days at a museum. For example, weekdays are generally less crowded and less hectic. However, some museums feature free admission on a certain day each week. If you do not like crowds, be prepared to pay admission and go on another weekday; free days are often more crowded with longer lines than even weekends. (Check out options for free admission on non-free days. For example, the Chicago Public Library provides to their patrons free admission passes to Chicago museums.)

Second, consider the time of day. Do not try to visit even the most exciting museum exhibit during your child's usual naptime. Avoid visits late in the day when your children may be tired or hungry. Make the museum experience a treat by paying attention to your children's regular schedules.

Third, think about the age of your children. Some museum curators recommend that very young children stay no more than an hour on each trip and that they ride in a stroller. That may mean that you will only see one or two permanent exhibits–preferably those with short lines or no lines. Nevertheless, remembering these simple tips may make the difference between an enjoyable time and a tiring day.

If your children are frequent visitors to a museum, they no doubt have favorite exhibits that they want to see on each trip. In order to be certain to include these exhibits and to visit other points of interest, it is a good idea to structure the visit so that younger children do not become too tired and older children do not get too bored. One way to do that is to construct an itinerary.

Creating an Itinerary

Creating a museum itinerary takes some planning. Visit the museum's Website or call for a packet of literature about the museum, its permanent exhibits and any new or visiting exhibits. You can find phone numbers for most museums in the yellow pages of the telephone book under the heading Museums. Gather as much information as you can—check local newspapers and publications about the arts and events in your area in addition to the museum information source itself.

Begin with the museum's physical layout. Using a blueprint layout provided or one you sketch yourself, start at the entrance and map out a walking route that allows you to see all the highlights plus anything you think your kids would relate to or find especially interesting. Do not forget to include as many interactive exhibits as possible; kids love to push buttons and watch the outcome (but be aware that you must watch younger children so that older, more aggressive kids do not prevent them from taking part).

If you have younger children, concentrate on the permanent exhibits where the lines are likely to be shorter and the din softer. Try to anticipate what will interest each child and the types of questions each one will ask. Skip those permanent exhibits that you think may be inappropriate for your younger children and move on to the next stop. And do not be surprised that the younger ones may be more interested in the museum's lights or plumbing than in the actual exhibit. Be ready to talk about whatever catches your youngsters' eyes.

Older kids have longer attention spans, so you can plan stops on the itinerary where you can linger at the exhibit. This is the time in the tour to distribute the note pads and pencils. Ask the kids to jot down first the most exciting part of the exhibit and second what they like best. Encourage them to add notes or expand on their notes. The more artistic ones may want to make a sketch. Do not make this seem like a school field trip; you simply want to help each child remember the highlights of each exhibit you visit.

If the museum offers audio tours, plan to outfit each of your older children with one. A good audio tour can emphasize the important points of everything you see. It is also a good idea to use one yourself. That way you will know what your children have learned and will be better able to fill in gaps or answer additional questions. Happily, the audio tape may answer many of your children's questions before they ask them—and some of your own as well.

As you continue to plan your itinerary, be sure to allow time for bathroom breaks and snack stops. Do not forget that many exhibits are very exciting, interactive or thought-provoking. Furthermore, crowds in an exhibit area may create a charged atmosphere. You want to avoid sensory overload, so incorporate some rests or breaks in the tour. Look on the museum map for seating areas or empty corners where you can retreat for a few minutes to talk about what you have just seen, what you are going to see or what may have been disturbing or perplexing to the children. Some museums have cafeterias or snack areas where you can take a snack break or eat a meal. You can also plan to end your tour with a snack treat before your start home.

Even if you have been walking and on your feet throughout your museum tour, your kids may need some time afterward to release pent-up energy. Allow time after you exit the museum for your kids to run around outside for a few minutes. Running and shouting are frowned upon in public museums, so plan to let your kids do both after the tour is finished. This is especially necessary if you face a long trip home.

Special Tour

If a full-day's tour at a museum is not appropriate or possible, there is another type of tour you can plan that may fit your needs. Arrange a museum treasure hunt. Again, you will need a map of the museum or at least familiarity with the layout and exhibits. Identify a famous or prominent item—a piece of equipment, a life exhibit, a painting or a constructed experiment—in each room of the museum and note it on a list. Arrange the list in the sequential order of the rooms in the museum. Begin the tour by giving a copy of the list to each child and explaining the object of the treasure hunt. As you visit each room, each child looks for the listed treasure in the room and check its off his or her list. The first child to find an object in a room wins a point for that room. After every child has located the treasure, you move as a group to the next room where the treasure hunt continues. At the end of the treasure hunt, the child with the most points is declared the winner and awarded a prize. The prizes do not need to be expensive or big; perhaps the winner can choose his seat on the trip home or request a special dish for supper. If you want, you can also bestow a small trinket or toy, but most kids are happy simply to be recognized as the winner.

The advantages of the museum treasure hunt approach are that it is a short tour, it requires everyone to visit every room (or as many as you want to include) in the museum, it introduces a sense of adventure and competition and it is fun. Plus, you can adjust the list to meet the ages and skill levels of the children. For example, you can ask your 3 year-old to find something red in a room while your 9 year-old looks for a specific painting. If your group includes children within a wide range of ages, you can even plan two levels of competition. You can always have more than one winner.

You may want to plan a treasure hunt tour for your first visit to a museum. The fact that you pass through every room provides an opportunity for you and your children to note exhibits they want to explore more fully on a future visit. This type of tour also reveals your children's interests so that you can plan future excursions that will interest them.

Because there are so many types of museums, you can plan many trips during the hot days of summer. Do not overlook small, specialized museums. Often, a town or neighborhood will have its own historical society or ethnic museum with exhibits pertaining to the area. Check the telephone book for small museums near your home. Give those that interest you a call so that you can plan your own tour before you visit the museum. You may find that a visit to a small museum can be an ideal way to while away a summer afternoon.

Resources

Visiting the Museum (Ages 4 to 8 years), (Puffin, 1992).

The Field Trip Handbook: A Guide for Visiting Museums. Grades K-8, (GoodYear Books, 1991).

Visit Google and search for the phrase: visiting museums with children. There are quite a few informative Websites, some of which describe specific museums in the United States and around the world.

29

Advanced
Card Games

A hot steamy day or a rainy interval calls out for a game of cards. All you need is a deck of cards and a comfortable spot to gather the players together. However, the day comes when the old fall back card game, Fish, is boring. It has become too easy and has been played too often. What can you suggest that will meet the requirements of being fun, being interesting and being educational?

There are several card games that are more advanced than fish and that appeal to older kids. Some expand on the basic premise of fish so the younger kids can easily learn them. Others, such as solitaire, teach the kids a new way of laying out cards. If you have preteens or teenagers, you may find that they are interested in learning how to play bridge. As you can see, there is a range of games here, from a game that requires one player (solitaire) to one that needs a minimum of four players (bridge). You and the kids may even want to set up a card tournament in which the kids and their friends play a variety of card games depending on their ages and abilities.

Here are a few suggestions to expand your kids' repertoire beyond Fish and 52 Pickup. The following descriptions will help you decide which games may appeal to your family; you should consult an authoritative reference for the complete set of rules. See Resources at the end of this chapter for more information. Solitaire is not included here because most kids have learned how to play it on the computer. All they have to do is substitute a deck of cards for the screen.

Authors

This is a more complicated version of fish, so it is a good game to use as a transition to more advanced games.

The object of this game, for three to six players, is to complete the most books—a book is a run of cards from ace to king occurring in the same suit which includes spades, hearts, clubs, or diamonds. The dealer distributes all the cards in the deck face down. Each player in turn asks an opponent for a specific card by rank and suit (for example, the king of hearts). If the opponent has the card, he or she must surrender it face up on the table. The player asking must have at least one card of that rank (king) in his hand. A player's turn continues as long as he receives the cards asked for. After that, the turn passes to the player on the left. Whenever a player completes a book, he shows it and then turns it face down on the table. The player with the most books at the end of the game is the winner.

Concentration

The is a memory game for two or more players. The object is to get as many pairs as possible; the winner is the player with the most pairs.

The dealer distributes all the cards one-by-one face down on the common card playing area so that the cards do not overlap. Each player in turn turns up any two cards, leaving the cards in their position on the table. If the cards are a match, the player takes them and turns up two more cards. If the cards are not a match, the player turns them face down, and the person on the left takes a turn. As the game progresses, the players remember where each card is and are able to turn over a matched pair during subsequent turns. The game ends when no cards remain on the table, and the winner is the player with the most pairs.

Crazy Eights

The object of this game, for three to four players, is to be the first player to run out of cards.

The dealer deals eight cards to each player, placing the remaining pile of cards face down on the table to form the draw pile. The first card in the draw pile is turned over to begin the discard pile. The players arrange the cards in their hands by suits. The first player must match the suit of the card facing up from the discard pile. The eights are wild. If an eight is played, that player names the suit to be played. If a player cannot follow suit, he must draw from the pile until he can play.

If a player uses up all the cards in the pile, the dealer places the top card on the pile face up and shuffles the rest to turn over as the pile. The winner is the player who runs out of cards first.

Uno

Similar to Crazy Eights, Uno uses it own double-deck set of cards with its own wild cards. In Uno the player has to match the number, color or symbol on the pile. Otherwise, the player draws from the pile. The wild or action cards include a reverse card, a skip card, a wild card and a wild card four card, each of which changes the action of the play. A player with only one card left in his hand must call out Uno or else draw two more cards from the pile. This penalty applies only if another player catches the first player failing to call out Uno. Once a player has run out of cards, the hand is over. This player receives points for all the other cards left in the opponents' hands. The first player to score 500 points wins.

Gin Rummy

The object of this game, usually played by two people, is to form the cards into sets, which is a sequence of cards according to suit or rank. Players must have a minimum of three cards in a suit or rank to start the combination called a meld.

The dealer distributes 10 cards to each player and places the remaining cards face down to form a draw pile. The first card in the pile is turned over to begin the discard pile. The first player can draw a card from either pile to try to fill out a set, but must discard a card to the discard pile. The player cannot discard the card he draws on the same turn.

A player can finish the game at any time, providing that any unmatched cards in the hand total fewer than 10 points (the ace is low in this game and worth one point, face cards are each worth 10 points and the other cards are face value). If a player can make all 10 cards in his hand into sets, he goes gin and his total unmatched card count is zero. The winner's score, however, is the total value of all the opponent's unmatched cards plus a 25-point bonus. The goal is to be the first player to score 100 points.

Other Games

There are numerous other card games your kids might enjoy, and you can thumb through card game books and other resources to find games that your kids can learn. Check out the rules for Double Solitaire, Hearts, Euchre, Pinochle and Canasta. You may find that the entire family will also enjoy playing these games, and you can arrange card marathons for summer evenings or vacation trips.

You will also need to decide whether or not some of the games are appropriate for your kids. For example, some teenagers may enjoy learning to play bridge, but this is a game that requires four players and a knowledge of the strategy of the game. Ideally, the best way to learn to play bridge is to do so with other experienced players who are able to teach it.

Poker, too, is popular among teens. There are many poker variations, so you can find a game that suits those players in your family. However, many teens have discovered online poker games that tie them to their computers and, in some cases, involve betting. You need to decide what kinds of limits you want to set when it comes to these types of online games.

Resources

The New Complete Hoyle Revised, (Doubleday, 1991).

This book is "the authoritative guide to the official rules of all popular games of skill and chance."

http://www.educationallearninggames.com/card-games.asp

This Website offers a catalog of educational kids' card games and family card games.

http://www.pixelpark.co.nz/card_games.htm

This Website provides family card games for players 8 years and older.

http://thehouseofcards.com/books.html

This Website features a catalog of card game books, including basic bridge, family card game collections, poker and rule books (*Hoyle's Rules of Games*).

30

Nature Activities:
A Window Box Garden

Most kids enjoy having their own personal piece of land to till, whether they live in an apartment or a house with a large yard. Older children with yards may want to stake out a patch of ground where they can grow whatever they choose. Younger children may find this to be daunting and lose interest. A child of any age, however, can enjoy planting a window box or other container because it is smaller in scope and easier to care for.

Type of Garden

Before you even select a box or container, sit down with your children and decide what kind of container garden they would like to grow. You do not have to plant only flowers. For instance, your kids might enjoy growing an herb or kitchen garden. Select herbs you use in your cooking, such as parsley, rosemary, chives, oregano or basil. Your gardener will love snipping off a fresh herb sprig for you to use in a favorite dish.

You could try planting small vegetables. Baby carrots, grape tomatoes, bib lettuce, or scallions do well in containers with full sun. Kids are pleased to add garnishes or salad ingredients from their gardens.

If a child is interested in health and fitness, suggest a medicine garden. The fluid from aloe vera leaves is famous for relieving skin irritations, abrasions, or minor burns. Peppermint and chamomile can be made into tea, and comfrey has been used to soothe minor cuts. All grow best in partial or full sun. Older children can use this kind of garden as a jumping-off point to study medicinal uses of other herbs and plants.

A desert garden appeals to many kids. Succulent plants, such as hens and chicks, aloe vera or jade plants grow well in full sun. Cacti come in so many different shapes, sizes and colors–some that even bloom–that children can have fun deciding which ones to plant.

An interesting alternative is a garden planted solely for its aromas. Many herbs have distinctive fragrances, and kids like to pinch or rub leaves and stems to release the interesting smells. Fragrant herbs include lavender, lemon balm, sage, peppermint and rosemary. You could also include these types of herbs in a kitchen herb garden if the container is large enough.

Finally, of course, is the old standard: a flower garden. Naturally, you should allow the children to select the flowers, but you can steer them toward choices that will look nice, grow well and require the kind of care your child is capable of giving. Encourage the kids to choose a variety of plants—tall plants, short plants, trailing vine plants and ground cover for filler. Color is also important. This may be a good opportunity to teach about complementary and contrasting colors, proportion (size of plants to size of container) and interesting planting patterns. And, of course, do not forget to tell your kids how to select plants that will thrive where you live. A delicate tropical vine may not do well if you live in northern Maine.

Here is a partial list of flowers and plants that can do well in containers:

- Petunias—petunias labeled multifloras have lots of blooms while cascading varieties add interest.
- Impatiens—low-growing dwarf types fulfill the requirement for short plants and all do well in shade.
- Sweet alyssum—can be both a trailer and a filler that often reseeds itself.
- Geraniums—have bright colors and are easy to grow.
- Miniature roses—provide varied colors and fragrance.
- Ground ivy—features very long green trailing stems that can survive some cold weather.

Choosing a Window Box

Selecting a window box or container is the next step. You want to choose a container of the right material, size and shape that will permit the plants you have selected to thrive. After all, no child will sustain interest in a window box if the plants fail to flourish or die.

The first consideration is drainage. Soil must drain water well and have space for air so there must be drainage holes. A lack of drainage holes or holes that are blocked slow drainage as does heavy or compacted soil. The result is water pooling at the bottom of the container, which can smother the roots and kill the plant. So look for containers with drainage holes. Some people also like to scatter pebbles in the bottom of the container to create air space around the plant roots.

The porosity of the container is also important. Porous containers permit moisture and air to enter more easily, but they dry out more quickly. This may be beneficial since the porosity not only cools the soil by evaporation thus allowing the roots to receive much-needed oxygen, but the porosity also draws off excess water therefore preventing waterlogged soil. On the other hand, nonporous containers hold the water better, which is better for some plants. Wood, paper pulp and unglazed pottery are porous containers, while plastic, metal and glazed pottery are nonporous containers.

You can follow a few simple rule for selecting a container's size and shape. When you buy a plant, place it into a container that is two inches deeper and two inches wider than its nursery container. You can also crowd plants more closely in containers than in the ground—crowding shortens the life span of plants, but a summer window box or container has a short life span anyway. In general, if the recommended spacing for a plant in the ground is 10 to 12 inches apart, you can space the plant 6 to 8 inches apart in a container. If a plant normally grows 10 to 12 inches tall, use a pot with a diameter of at least 8 inches.

Note: Obtaining a plant container does not mean you have to drive to the nearest nursery and spend a great deal of money to find exactly the right container for your child's garden. You and your child can use your imaginations to look for something a little different or readily available. A hollow log from the woods, an old wooden or metal bucket, mismatched mixing bowls, kitchen canisters, old boots, an outgrown doll carriage or an inner tube—all of these choices will work. Just check for drainage holes and for appropriate size.

You should discuss all of these container characteristics with the children gardeners if they are old enough to understand the science behind the requirements. This is an opportunity for both science lessons in understanding botanic physiology and math lessons in calculating container sizes.

Planting the Garden

Planting is the fun part for kids—they get to dig in dirt, slosh water about and get muddy. Let them do all the work. Explain what needs to be done and stand back. The kids can plant directly into the container, or you can fill the container with plants in pots, using moss, bark or dirt to fill in the spaces around the pots. The advantage of this method is that your gardener can remove and replace individual pots if a plant begins to straggle or dies. Whichever method you select, first check for drainage holes before pouring dirt into the container. Help your children design the arrangement of plants by setting the individual plants on top of the soil to view the overall effect. Basically, a window box that will be attached to a window frame or a fence should have taller plants in the back, shorter plants in the middle and trailers at the front so that vines cascade over the front of the box. Look, too, for a pleasing distribution of color.

Show your children how to dig holes for the plants, using a trowel or a large kitchen spoon. Most children, especially young ones, are more adept and comfortable with the kitchen spoon. When the plants are resting in their holes, have the children firmly press the dirt around the soil. Be sure to leave at least one inch at the top for watering.

The last step is watering the plants. Do not let the children overwater, but show them how to make certain that the soil is uniformly moist. A watering can is best, since a garden hose may displace the soil or knock over the plants. Of course, you can always use the hose to wash off the gardeners after the job is done.

Now is the time to stress to the children that a container garden is not one afternoon's work. They will need to tend their garden throughout the growing season by watering and grooming to remove droopy or dead blooms, leaves or stems. Show the children how to test the soil in the container every day with their fingers to see if they need to water. If the soil is dry an inch below the surface, it is time to water. Emphasize as well to the children that pinching off dead blooms and trimming leaves and stems to shape the plant will help the plant grow. Just leave at least two thirds of the plant intact.They should also be on the lookout for bugs and pests. If you notice pests, show the children how to remove any affected leaves and to spray the plants with water to get rid of the bugs. Do not let the children use commercial insecticides; many are toxic if inhaled or absorbed through the skin.

You now have a mini-garden that you and your young gardeners can enjoy all summer. The kids have the satisfaction of creating something beautiful and alive, and you have the sense of accomplishment of helping them learn about plants and their care. Plus, this is one project that will continue to bring pleasure all summer long.

Resources

Container Gardening: Creating Style and Beauty with Containers, (Home Improvement/Gardening Editors of Creative Publishing International, 2000).

Complete Container Garden, (Readers Digest, 2003).

www.windowbox.com

This Website offers tips on planting and maintaining container gardens. This is also a source of plants and other supplies.

www.flowerframers.com/createwindowboxgarden.htm

This Website also provides tips on container gardening, including a section on frequently asked questions (FAQs).

31
Exploring the Neighborhood

Exploring your own neighborhood is an opportunity to teach your kids how to read maps, recognize architectural features and understand the importance of history to an area. The advantage of this activity is that it is concrete and personal—you are not reading or talking about an abstract concept or a faraway place. You are talking about home.

Getting Started

Before you actually begin to explore your neighborhood, you and your kids should define the parameters of what you consider to be your neighborhood. A basic definition could designate a neighborhood as an area that is smaller than a town but larger than a city block, in which people live together. However, you will need to adjust this definition to fit your location. If you live in a large city, a small town or a rural area, your neighborhood may be confined to the area through which you can walk or drive. A neighborhood in a populous urban area, for example, may be one square block while a rural neighborhood may encompass the miles that stretch between homes. In your own case, however, a neighborhood may be the boundaries within which your kids are allowed to roam.

Using Maps

Start with a map of your country, state and city. You can use a road atlas or an encyclopedia—but better yet, use a globe. Your goal is to help the kids understand where their neighborhood fits into the world. The next step—looking at a map of your specific neighborhood—is fun. There are several Websites you will want to visit. Begin with Mapquest *(www.mapquest.com)* or Google Maps *(www.google. com/maps)*.

After entering your address into either Mapquest or Google Maps, you will see a map of your home and the surrounding area. You can help the kids zoom into the map or out of it and move in any of the four directions to get a sense of the larger area. This is your chance to show the kids how to read a map. In addition, refer to the road atlas and its map legends and symbols as well. If you have younger children who are not yet ready to read maps, perhaps this is your opportunity to teach them their address and phone number.

Next, visit TerraServer-USA *(www.terraserverusa.com)*. When you enter your address (have your younger kids call out their address), you will have a choice of an aerial, topographic, or urban map. Look at all three. The aerial map shows your home and street as well as several surrounding streets or areas. The topographic map indicates land features of your neighborhood. But the urban map will fascinate the kids. This photo is a bird's eye view that you can zoom into and out of to see individual buildings in more detail. Depending on when the map was taken, your kids may even see your own car parked in your driveway. Let the kids rove over the map, looking for landmarks such as their school, their friends' houses, area stores, the library or the nearby park.

While you are still looking at the map, note the streets and highways. Usually, streets and roads are built first in a neighborhood. The map will show the kids whether or not your community's street system is built on a grid or if the streets follow natural boundaries such as rivers, streams or hills. Much of a neighborhood's character and layout depends on its topography. Sometimes even the names of neighborhoods, such as Riverside or Beverly Hills, indicate the origin of the area. Some towns that were carved out of a forest or wooded area have street names such as Elm, Maple, Hickory or Oak. Other neighborhoods have streets named after the original Native American tribes or the first settlers. Often, the layout and names of an area reflect its geography and history.

Touring the Neighborhood

Use a printout of the urban bird's eye view map to plan your next step—a tour of the neighborhood. Walking or bicycling is the best way to see the neighborhood. Plus, this will give you a chance to talk to neighbors and visitors to the neighborhood. If you carry along a copy of a topographic map from the TerraServerUSA Website or from the U.S. Geological Survey *(www.usgs.gov)*, you can pick out hills, streams or ponds, roads or other prominent physical features. During your walk, have the kids examine the soil (sand, clay, loam or rock) and the types of vegetation. Ask the kids to guess from looking at the soil and other topographical features if they think the area was originally a woods, a farm, a valley or a port. Is your neighborhood old (tall, mature trees, for example) or is part of your neighborhood a newer development? You may have to include a stop at your neighborhood library to learn the answers to some of these questions.

Direct the kids' attention to the buildings and architecture of the neighborhood. What are most of the buildings constructed from? Wood, brick or half and half? Are the homes the same age, or are some houses old with newer construction added later? Is there one definite architectural style? Is your community composed primarily of single-family homes, or are there multiple-family units and apartment complexes?

Is there a commercial zone in your neighborhood? If so, take the kids through this area and look at it from a perspective different from that of a customer or shopper. For instance, do many of the employees at the stores or offices live in your locale, or do the workers travel into your neighborhood to work? If many workers drive to your neighborhood to work, does that affect the transportation system or the streets and roads? If you do not want to ask these questions directly, go to the library and research the census information for the area.

Encourage your kids to talk to local shopkeepers, pharmacists, grocery store managers, bookstore owners or anyone else who lives or works in your neighborhood. Visit city hall or the local library and talk to the people who work there. It is important that the kids hear others' perspectives of the neighborhood; they will develop a more accurate overall sense of the area, and they may begin to understand the impact local officials can have on a neighborhood. They will also begin to see the value of friendly conversations with neighbors as a way to make new friends and to draw people in the vicinity together. The custom of greeting your neighbors from your front porch or backyard slowly disappeared as everyone drifted indoors to watch television or use the computer. Exploring your neighborhood with the kids is a good beginning to learning how to live in a community again.

In your travels around the neighborhood, do not forget to visit the areas the kids know best: the schools and the parks. This time let them show you what they think are the most important highlights. Ask if anyone knows a special place on the school grounds. Which is the best slide on the playground? Is there an especially lumpy patch of grass on the baseball diamond in the park? What needs to be done to make the park a more inviting place? The kids will appreciate your asking, and you may be surprised at their thoughtful answers.

Recording Your Neighborhood Exploration

Because learning about your neighborhood is an ongoing activity—and because a community continually undergoes change and growth—keeping a journal of what you learn about the area is a good idea. Equip the kids with loose-leaf notebooks, pencils and a camera. The type of camera—either disposable or digital—will depend on the age and ability of your kids. Have them maintain an ongoing journal of sights they see and facts they learn. Tuck in copies of the maps your have accumulated, and encourage the kids to add brochures, ads, sale flyers, public notices and other mementos they pick up out in the neighborhood. The journal will function as a reflection of the neighborhood—even as it changes—and you may be surprised at how often someone in the family returns to the journal to refresh their memory of the neighborhood.

Resources

www.usgs.gov

> The is the official Website of the U.S. Geological Survey, which offers a wide variety of information about the physical and topographic features of land, neighborhoods, towns, and regions in the United States.

http://nationalmap.gov

> This is another government Website with informational maps of all areas in the United States.

http://gsc.nrcan.gc.ca/map/index_e.php

> This Website is the Canadian equivalent of *www.usgs.gov*.

Exploring Our World: Neighborhoods and Communities (Grades 1-3), (Scholastic, 1999).

> This book focuses on exploring neighborhoods and communities and includes a play, a game board, literature links, mapping instructions, a pull-out poster and other activities.

On the Town: A Community Adventure, (Greenwillow, 2002).

> Geared toward preschool level, this is a story about a boy and his mother who explore their community and get to know the people living there.

Mapping Penny's World, (Owlet Paperbacks, 2003).

> This book presents mapmaking skills through a fictional account of a young girl and her dog.

32
Camping

Family camping is fun for kids—and parents, too—if you take some time to plan your trip. There are many advantages to family camping:

- Camping is affordable. And if you do not want to invest in camping gear until you know for sure whether or not your family will become camping enthusiasts, you can borrow or rent what is required on an as-needed basis.
- Camping allows flexible planning; you can camp for 1 night or for 2 weeks; you can camp near home or far away.
- Camping permits a real change of pace from your everyday schedule; from lowering your cleanliness standards to living without electricity are just two of the many ways you can escape from the daily routine.
- Camping allows you and your kids to try new activities such as hiking, canoeing and outdoor cooking.
- Camping is a way to introduce your kids to nature and the environment.

Getting Started

If your family has not camped before, you may want a trial run before you commit to a week-long trip. Why not begin in your own backyard? Setting up camp in your own yard allows a test run consisting of activities such as pitching a tent and sleeping outdoors. And, of course, there is the added advantage of home as a safety net in case bad weather or some other problems occur.

If your kids seem ready to camp farther away from home, you can try car camping; that is, setting up the tent and campsite beside the car at a site in a campground or state park. The car functions as a safety net in the event that the weather does not cooperate or the kids feel safer in an enclosed vehicle.

Either one of these trial runs—or both—should give you some idea why camping is such a popular family activity. If the kids are eager to camp, are willing to help out and are enthusiastic about exploring the outdoors, then you can look into the camping opportunities in your area.

Planning the Camping Trip

There are four requirements for planning a camping trip: 1) campground type, 2) campground facilities, 3) distance from campground to town and, 4) the seasonal weather.

Campground Type

Most first-time campers are tent campers, so you will want to locate a campground that caters to families with tents. Look for nearby campgrounds that are either privately owned or that are operated by county, state or national parks. A good resource is *Woodall's North American Campground Directory,* (Woodall Publishing, 2007). You can also contact the parks and recreation department for your state to ask about local and regional campgrounds.

Campground Facilities

Once you have selected some possible campsites, contact the campground to find out what sort of facilities and amenities each one offers. Questions concerning a site's basic facilities could include the following: Is there safe drinking water or will you have to carry your own or bring along a water purifier or filter? Are there showers and restrooms? Or will you be using pit toilets? If, indeed, pit toilets are the only facilities, be sure to tell your kids about them. Warn the children that pit toilets may not smell nice and they may be dark inside. This is the time to add a flashlight for each person to your equipment list.

You will also want to find out about each campsite's amenities. Some campgrounds have a children's playground or swimming pool. You may want to consider a campground with these amenities for your first outing even though you will not really be roughing it. If you have older kids, you may prefer access to a lake for fishing or to a stream for canoeing. Do not forget to find out if you need a license and if you can rent equipment.

Distance from Campground to Town

This is an important factor to consider because a nearby town provides the resources to purchase anything you forget, the facilities to handle an emergency or illness and the retreat when the weather makes camping impossible. One of the secrets of successful family camping is knowing when to throw in the towel and take advantage of an escape route.

Seasonal Weather

Weather is the main reason camping trips succeed or fail. There are advantages to camping in each season, but summer weather is the most likely to be predictable.

Yes, it does rain, but the rain does not change to sleet. And, yes, it may be hot, but you can look for a shaded campsite and provide shelter and screens. Naturally, you will check the weather forecasts before you leave so that you can avoid at least the most extreme weather. Be sure you are prepared to handle changes in weather; in that way, your trip should be a happy experience.

Camping Gear

There are three simple criteria for a successful camping trip: shelter, food and entertainment. You do not have to complicate the packing with unnecessary gear; after all, the idea is to get away as a family to enjoy some time together.

Shelter

To provide shelter, you will need a tent, sleeping bags, air mattresses and perhaps a dining canopy or shade covering. Choose a tent that will accommodate the family comfortably when everyone sleeps and also when everyone is forced by rain to hang out in the tent for a few hours. Be sure the tent has a floor stitched to the walls a few inches up from the ground. This keeps rain or moisture from seeping in through the seam at ground level. Also, select a tent that you can easily set up. Unless your kids are older, you may be erecting the tent by yourself.

Choose sleeping bags that are warm yet ventilated. You will also need a pad or air mattress under each bag to cushion the sleeper on hard ground. Be sure each child can operate the zipper on his or her bag.

A canopy can be installed over a table to provide shade or protection from rain while you eat or play games. Some canopies are equipped with screens to keep insects from spoiling your fun.

Finally, pack clothing for everyone that can be layered and then peeled way as the wearer gets warm or added as the wearer becomes cold. Remember, even on the warmest day, the evening may be cool.

Food

This is not the time to experiment with gourmet cooking. Pack the basics, including ice coolers, a skillet, a pot, metal utensils, flatware and dishwashing supplies. Use paper plates, paper towels and a paper or plastic tablecloth. Bring plenty of trash bags–you want to maintain a clean campsite, and if you are in a wilderness area, you must carry out all the trash you generate. Campgrounds have trash receptacles, but you must package your garbage to prevent bugs and odors.

Plan simple meals. Canned foods, finger foods, hot dogs, or precooked meals are all good. Juice in individual boxes are fine for kids and you will want to be certain that everyone drinks enough water. You can carry your own, bring along a filter or depend on the campground for a water source. This is why you want to be near a town so that you can buy anything you forget or use up.

Entertainment

If your campground offers swimming, hiking, canoeing, bicycling or nature programs, you have built-in entertainment. If you want to provide your own, pack a deck of cards, a favorite board game, a few books (do not forget a book about stars or astronomy and a book about nature) or craft equipment. You will have abundant craft materials at your feet—twigs, leaves, acorns, moss and rocks.

Other Essentials

Every camping family must have a first-aid kit, matches, sunscreen, flashlights (for the bathroom or shadow puppet shows on tent walls), whistles (for each child to signal distress if he or she wanders away) and simple hiking gear (water canteen, dry socks and a compass).

Safety

Safety is crucial, especially when you are camping. Before you even leave home, tell someone where you are going and when you expect to return. Do the same when you strike out on a hike or walk. Have each child wear a whistle and carry water when leaving the campsite. Never hike alone and never allow young children to wander out of sight. Teach your kids to look before they step over logs or a mound of grass or leaves. If you or your kids get lost, remain where you are, blow your whistle and wait. If you told someone where you were going, they will hunt for you when you do not return.

Careful planning will help to ensure that family camping trips are an enjoyable way to spend time together.

Resources

Camping With Kids, (Wilderness Press, 2005).

> This book provides the basics of family camping for beginners or experienced campers. The book covers car, tent or RV camping and also describes related activities such as backpacking, canoeing or other extended trips.

Cooking on a Stick, (Gibbs, Smith Publisher, 2000).

> This book discusses everything you need to know about campfire cookery, including building a fire, cooking without pots and pans and creating recipes on the trail.

Finding
New Parks

Looking for a new park is an undertaking that can be as simple as walking or driving through your neighborhood or as complex as searching for a special theme park for a day trip.

Neighborhood Parks

You may have already discovered a new park on one of your nature walks or while exploring your neighborhood. However, you may be unaware of other parks in the area, particularly if you have a large yard where your kids spend most of their time. One of the best ways to discover parks and other recreational facilities in your area is to take a ride on your bicycles or in the car to see what is available.

A good-sized park is apparent when you tour a neighborhood, but many urban and suburban areas take advantage of unused land by tucking in pocket parks or green areas. These parks are not always so visible from regularly traveled streets and therefore may be uncrowned. If there is enough space, the municipality may install a small tot lot with a few swings, a slide, climbing equipment or a sandbox. Even those parks with no equipment may offer an appealing spot to enjoy a picnic lunch or play a game of tag.

Larger parks may have playground equipment, but additional amenities may be available as well such as a swimming pool, tennis courts or ball fields. Some boast a field house and staff who plan activities and events for the neighborhood kids. If you find such a park near your neighborhood, stop in and ask about enrolling your kids in summer activities. It may be worth the expense because such facilities often offer equipment and programs you cannot duplicate at home. Ask, too, about neighborhood events that take place in the park. Are there parades or picnics on holidays, such as the Fourth of July? Are there regular games and playoffs of sports teams? What about music concerts in the evening? Some parks arrange for local musicians to perform on a regular basis in the early evening and encourage families to bring a picnic and lawn chairs to enjoy the concert while dining.

To find out about the parks in your area, contact your nearest municipality or county headquarters and ask to speak to someone in the parks and recreation department. Also, you may be able to gather information on area parks by locating these government offices online.

Other sources of park information can be obtained by contacting chambers of commerce or real estate agencies. Both of these resources make a point to promote local attractions and facilities in order to attract business. Review their Websites, or when phoning, ask them to direct you to more information about the parks and recreational facilities in your area.

Exploring a Neighborhood Park

A park can offer more than just playgrounds and other amenities. It can provide information about the neighborhood. When you and your kids visit a park for the first time, take a close look at the features of it. Seek out monuments, statues and plaques to become better informed about the neighborhood. Once you learn about a famous event or person by having read the plaques on the monuments and statues, you may want to conduct additional research into the history of the region.

Have the kids make a note of the trees, foliage, soil and the topographic features of the park. This will give them an idea of the natural history of the region. Begin your park visit with some questions:

- What do the kids think they will discover on a nature walk through a neighborhood park?
- Do the trees that grow in the park also grow in your backyard?
- Is the soil rocky?
- Is the park hilly?
- Are these features representative of the area as a whole?
- Are the paths or walkways paved? If so, what was used to pave the paths or build fences in the park?
- Are the same materials in the paths and fences used in the homes in the neighborhood? If so, does that mean that the natural resources of the area have determined the architectural style of the buildings in the area?

It is amazing to discover how much you can learn about a locale by just strolling through its parks.

Other Types of Parks

One of the tasks you can assign to your older kids is to find out about parks that offer adventures or programs for an afternoon or a day. You may be surprised at the wide variety of day trips you and the kids can take without breaking the budget or traveling too far.

You should first decide what kind of adventure you want to have and then how far you want to go, how long you want to be gone, and how much you want to spend. Selecting your adventure may not be as easy as you think since there may be many different programs available, depending of course on where you live.

For example, you can select hiking, mountain climbing, horseback riding, mountain biking, rafting, tubing or fishing. There are half-day or full-day sessions for many of these activities, and the programs can be found all over the country. A good place to start researching this is at GORPTravel *(http://gorptravel.away. com/day-trips.html)*. This Website lists day-trip opportunities by type of activity and location.

And if you live near a body of water, you will appreciate the information at this site which provides details on whale watching in the Pacific Ocean, sailing on lakes and kayaking on seas, rivers and streams. You can also search for longer vacations and educational programs in the national parks.

National and State Parks

You may be aware of the primary national parks, but you and your kids can go online to find out which ones are closest to you and what they offer. State parks may be a little different. Like the pocket parks in towns and suburbs, small state parks may be so well hidden that you are unaware of their existence. Visit your state Website to learn about the parks and recreation department. You may find that there is a small state park with a range of activities and accommodations that would appeal to your family.

Amusement or Theme Parks

An amusement or theme park features rides and other attractions designed to entertain large groups of people. An amusement park is more elaborate than a simple city park or playground and can be expensive and crowded. Nevertheless, a day at an amusement park can be a highlight of the summer.

If you do not have the time, money or access to a large amusement park, look around your neighborhood for a temporary amusement park with mobile rides and booths—often called a fun fair or carnival. Some municipalities set up carnivals for holidays or civic events, or you may find one sponsored by local merchants to attract shoppers to a shopping mall.

Theme parks are more focused forms of amusement parks. Many are year-round facilities that try to convey the sense that visitors are in a different place or time. Often a theme park will have various sections of the park devoted to historical periods, fairy tales or stories. On the other hand, you may find smaller theme parks with less elaborate rides that will suit your younger children. In general, most theme parks are permanent entertainment parks created to provide a fun-filled day for all ages. Nevertheless, you need to consider your kids' ages, interests and abilities before you spend the time and money to visit a theme park that may not be appropriate for everyone in your family.

As a part of your summer activities, planning a trip with your kids to an amusement or theme park will probably be a special treat. You can plan a day trip if you live near one of these parks. Or a visit to this type of park may become a part of a longer family vacation.

Resources

www.nps.gov

> This is the official Website of the United States National Park Service. This site is geared toward parents, teachers and kids and will help you locate a park as well as find additional information.

http://usparks.about.com/od/stateparksus/State_Parks_of_the_United_States.htm

> This Website describes the U.S. state parks system including maps, events and contact information. There is also information on the best state parks as rated by the directors of the state parks system.

http://bestentertainment.tv/Entertainment/4/ThemeParks/themeparks/Theme-Parks.html

> This Website provides links to theme and amusement parks including references to Disney, Six Flags and local parks.

www.ultimaterollercoaster.com/themeparks/locator/idx_location.mpl

> This Website offers a directory to theme and amusement parks categorized by state. The site also includes information about and directions to nearby lodging.

Learning
How to Fish

Learning how to fish can be the beginning of a life-long hobby. Teaching children how to fish introduces them to nature and the outdoors even if they do not pursue the activity as a hobby later on. Kids today are more in touch with their computer and cell phone than they are with the outdoors. Yet fishing teaches kids about being stewards of nature so that they can understand issues such as preventing water pollution and maintaining the balance of nature.

In keeping with this kind of thinking, many fishermen today release the fish they catch so that fishing is more of a sport and skill rather than a means of obtaining food. Still, there is some value in occasionally taking fish home to eat: Children can see the interdependence of living creatures. Plus, they learn that food does not just come in plastic wrappings from the grocery store.

Getting Started

Keep it Simple

This is the basic rule for your first fishing outing. Your kids are interested in fun and spending time with you. Trying to maneuver complicated equipment at the same time as they are learning the pros and cons of specialized bait will just be frustrating for them. You can have a good time with a cane pole, a hook, a bobber and some bait.

Keep it Short

Kids, especially very young ones, have short attention spans. A good rule of thumb is to plan a fishing trip to last 1-hour per each year of the child's age. If your kids vary significantly in age, take along toys and games to occupy the younger ones while older kids continue to fish. It never pays to force a child to participate in anything longer than his or her attention span dictates.

Take the time to plan your first fishing trip. And encourage your kids to help. Take them along to buy a fishing license (you may be able to buy a 24-hour one-time use license at country offices, bait and tackle shops, sporting goods stores or even online). Once you have selected your fishing trip destination, pull out a map and have the kids plot the route to the site. When you arrive, give them some time to reconnoiter, looking for good fishing spots, places to dig worms and places for a picnic lunch. Some kids enjoy exploring their surroundings as much as actually fishing.

If possible, locate a fishing spot that is easy to get to, has accessible rest rooms, provides clean drinking water and, as a bonus, features a playground. Some places also offer a pay-per-fish option whereby you pay for each fish you catch from a stocked pond or lake. This ensures your kids of a catch the first time out. Plan to go in the morning; the fish seem to bite better then and the kids are full of energy.

On the other hand, if you cannot find such a fishing spot near your home, you and the kids can have a good time with simple equipment and bait at a nearby stream or pond. Call around to tackle stores to ask where the fish are biting. Remember, too, that kids do not usually care about the size of the fish they catch as much as they care about just catching something.

A word of caution: Do not forget to set up a backup plan. If the weather changes, your equipment breaks or the kids get bored, have an alternative activity in mind.

Equipment and Supplies

Each child will need a fishing pole. You can buy reasonably priced children's rod and reel combinations or simple cane poles. The pole should fit the child's hands and be as long as your child is tall. The pole will need a string tied to one end with a hook and bobber at the end of the string. The hook holds the bait, and the bobber keeps the bait and hook near the surface of the water where the fish bite. Kids love to watch for the bobber to bob up and down, signifying that you have a bite. If your kids are young, you may want to debarb the hooks by pressing the barb against the hook's shaft with needle-nose pliers.

Use live bait—earthworms, minnows or crickets are the best for beginners. You can buy bait, but many kids like to dig for earthworms. Keep worms in a closed container inside a cooler to keep them fresh. If you buy minnows, keep them in a bucket of cool water and use a net to scoop them out. It is your call about whether or not you bait the hook or let the kids do it. Many kids love to bait the hook, while others back off. You will have to play this one by ear and be prepared to take over if necessary.

While this basic equipment is all that you need to get started, you will also want to bring along other supplies. You will need a cooler to hold your cold drinks, lunch and bait. Snacks, sunscreen and insect repellents are also required. And be sure to take along a first-aid kit with supplies to treat scrapes, cuts and bites and include waterless hand soap and some clean rags to wipe off hands.

Finally, do not forget the camera. This is one memory you will want to add to the family fun album.

Safety

Safety comes first in any activity with your kids. This is especially true when you are fishing. All children should wear personal flotation devices in the water, on the shore or on a boat. Establish hard and fast rules around the water and make certain your kids understand the rules and the reasons for them. If you have a group of children, set up a buddy system, so that no one is ever alone.

Be diligent about fluid consumption. Hot summer temperatures can lead to fluid depletion and even heat stroke. Kids may not notice that they are thirsty, so offer cool water and other drinks often. Also, sweating washes away sunscreen and insect repellant; replenish these as the day wears on. You may want to spray repellent onto clothing rather than skin to ensure longer-lasting protection.

What to Do if You Catch a Fish

What are your options if the kids are successful and catch a fish on their first time out? A hooked fish is still alive, so your first consideration may be to answer the catch-and-release question. Rivers and streams in some areas are subject to catch-and-release regulations if certain game fish are threatened with extinction or depletion. This information may be posted, or you may learn about the restrictions when you buy the fishing license. In this case, you must explain the rules to the kids and help them release the fish back into the waterway.

On the other hand, if there are no restrictions, you may still want to discuss the catch-and-release option with your kids. You can suggest that you take the fish home for dinner or that you release it back into its habitat. Some kids may have mixed feelings about this, in which case you should make the decision. You can give the kids the option of releasing the fish or waiting to see if you catch enough fish to make a meal. Whatever you do, make it clear that it is not sportsmanlike to kill a fish unless you intend to eat it.

If you do release the fish, wet your hands and hold the fish firmly behind its head with one hand while gripping the hook in the other hand and pushing it back through the fish's lip. Hold the fish under water while doing this and then gently slide it off into the water.

If you decide to take the fish home, run a stringer hook through the fish's bottom jaw and slip it back into the water to keep it alive while you continue to fish. Or you can sever the fish's spinal cord behind its head and store it on ice. Be sure to identify and measure the fish and then snap a photo of the young fisherman holding her catch.

Resources

www.fishingworld.com

This Website has tips for taking kids fishing plus links to other useful sites about fishing with kids.

www.fishingworks.com/kids_fishing/index.cfm

This Website provides instructions on teaching kids how to fish. There are also links to other articles and information about fishing with kids in Canada.

www.kansasangler.com/kidstips.html

This Website lists FAQs from both adults and kids about fishing. There are also safety tips and information about fishing derbys.

www.bwca.cc/activities/fishing/kidsfishing.html

This Website from Boundary Waters Canoe Area offers guidelines on getting kids started fishing.

Fishing for Kids: A Family Fishing Guide, (Northword Press, 1993).

This book introduces the techniques, equipment and bait used to catch various types of fish.

Gone Fishing with Kids: How to take your kid fishing and still be friends, (Gone Fishin Enterprises, 1997).

This book looks at the psychological aspects of fishing with kids as well as the practicalities of fishing. This is a good reference book for parents who have no fishing experience.

Nature Hike

A nature walk can be eye-opening to everyone–from budding naturalists and scientists to parents who are trying to open up new vistas to their children. A nature hike can be as simple as a short stroll through your own yard or as elaborate as a planned activity at a nearby park, botanic garden or beach. In either case, being alert to your surroundings can provide you with a new understanding of nature and the environment.

Planning a Nature Hike

Outings are more enjoyable when planning takes place. First, tell your kids what to expect. Explain that they are going to observe nature and that they may see some unusual sights. Then describe some details about where they are going (for example, it will involve a long car ride, there will be a park nearby with a playground or there will be no bathroom facilities).

Plan short hikes in the beginning until you can assess each child's interest and perseverance. If any of the kids are quite young, you may end up carrying them on a long hike, and that wears out both you and the kids. Pack a backpack–ideally, a backpack for each child that contains the following items:

- Snacks (trail mix–what else?)
- Water
- A small notebook
- Paper and crayons (to make bark or rock etchings)
- Pencils
- A magnifying glass
- Small plastic bags (to collect specimens)
- Larger plastic bags (to tote out your own trash)
- Waterless soap or wipes
- Paper towels

Anything that you use, including food leftovers, wipes or paper towels, must be carried home or disposed of properly. This is an excellent opportunity to teach the kids about keeping the wilderness clean.

Emphasize the importance of safety to the kids. Have the kids wear bright colors and if you are going to be on a wilderness trail, equip yourself and each child with a whistle. You might want to establish a buddy system if there are several children on the trip. You can also carry a cell phone, but you may end up somewhere where you have spotty or no service. Above all, emphasize to the children that they must not wander away and must be in touch with you at all times.

Guiding the Hike

You do not have to be a naturalist to take your kids on a nature hike. Just look for opportunities to observe something new or unusual. Start by asking the kids to look at the ground and note what they see. Then have them look at the sky, into the trees or at the underside of a cliff. Ask them to focus on the weather and how it affects nature. Let them make their own observations and ask questions.

Encourage the kids to use all of their senses; watch for different colors, smells and textures. Look for layers and varied colors in rocks. How does the bark on one tree differ from the bark on another? Ask the kids to differentiate between the odors of grasses, dirt, bark or wild flowers. Collect different kinds of specimens–pebbles, soil, leaves or bark–and put them into small plastic bags to take home to analyze. But remember, you cannot remove anything from state or national parks, and if you are exploring on private property, be sure to obtain permission from the owner before gathering specimens.

After you have examined the differences in natural objects, try to steer the kids toward seeing all the parts of nature as connected. How does one part of the system affect another? Does the density of a tree's leaf canopy affect the plants growing below it? How does rain change the environment and its inhabitants? How do animals and bugs use camouflage to fit in and protect themselves from danger? Your goal is to guide your kids to observe nature from the particular to the whole.

Look for evidence of wild animals. Is there a path with animal foot prints? Can you follow ants to their anthill? Who can find nests in a tree, hidden in a log or under foliage? Who can hear the rustle of leaves caused by a scurrying chipmunk or squirrel? Can you hear more than one kind of bird calling or singing?

Do not overlook streams, ponds or even a puddle. Before you leave home, cut off the bottom of a paper or plastic milk carton. Cover the bottom opening with heavy plastic wrap, extending the wrap halfway up the side of the carton. Secure the wrap with a rubber band. Open or cut off the top of the carton so that you can look through the top and out the bottom. When you find a pond or a puddle, push the carton viewer halfway down into the water. Look through the plastic on the bottom of the carton to view life in the water. You can see bugs, dirt, leaves and whatever else is on the bottom including tiny fish.

Is someone writing everything down in a notebook? Keeping a journal of what they see is an important task for the kids, because a nature hike will most likely raise questions that require research in order to answer them. So you will want each child to be prepared to look up information in the library or online based on what he or she records in a notebook. This tends to become a circular exercise: The kids look up what they saw, which, in turn, creates more questions that can be answered by going on another nature hike. The key here is the act of discovering as opposed to merely observing.

Trying Something Different

Once you have hooked your kids on discovering the mysteries of nature, you can suggest different kinds of nature walks.

The Silent Walk

Instruct the kids to take a nature hike without talking or making any noise. Most will enjoy the challenge of walking in a natural area without stepping on twigs or leaves. The goal of the walk is to listen for every sound of nature. Have them concentrate on listening and recording what they hear in their journal. Or they can create a map of the area on which they draw symbols or pictures representing the sounds they hear. When they are finished, they will have a sound map of the area. To make it more interesting move on to another area and draw another sound map. How do the two maps differ?

Blindfolded Walk

Pair off the kids and have one blindfold the other. With a partner to serve as a guide, each child can take a nature walk, using the senses of sound, smell and touch to map out each walk. Have the kids take turns so that everyone wears the blindfold for a portion of the walk. The child without the blindfold can stop and write down the observations of the blindfolded partner to compare with his own observations later.

Night Nature Walk

A nature walk after dark can be a totally different experience. While similar to the blindfolded walk because of limited vision in the darkness, this type of adventure is nevertheless different because of the types of activities occurring in the nighttime setting. For example, you may see a different set of animals–those known as nocturnal creatures–who begin their day after the light is gone. Listen for owls and look for bats. Study the stars. Urge your kids to make mental notes for their journal, since they will be unable to see to be able to write in the dark.

Conservation Nature Walk

Talk to your kids about how they can help the environment by making cleanup part of their nature walks. Since you are carrying a plastic bag to cleanup after yourselves on your walk, remind the kids that they can also remove litter and other trash that does not belong in natural areas. Issue disposable gloves or work gloves to each child, and show them what to pick up and toss into their garbage bags. This can be done on a walk in the park, in a natural habitat, on a beach or even during a city nature walk. You can even go a step further and help the kids identify recyclable items in the trash to dump into recycle bins. This task should not distract the kids from their nature study, but it does instill in them a respect for nature and the environment.

Resources

www.our-kids.com/nature_centers.shtml

> This Website provides locations and descriptions of nature centers that offer nature hikes for kids.

www.wvdnr.gov/Wildlife/Hike.shtm

> Visit this Website to understand how to plan an un-nature hike in order to learn about adaptation and camouflage in nature.

Take a City Nature Walk, (Stillwater Publishing, 2005).

> This book, geared toward children between the ages of 9 and 12, points out what to look for on a nature walk in an urban environment.

Take a Tree Walk, (Stillwater Publishing, 2002).

> This book offers clues to identifying trees and is a good companion on nature walks, playground outings and car trips.

All About Birds

One of the easiest ways to introduce your kids to nature and the enjoyment of the outdoors is to encourage them to become birdwatchers. Birdwatching requires kids to take a panoramic view of nature. They will be looking into the sky, into trees, into bushes and into all the areas in between. It is a hobby–or even better, a habit–in which they can participate anywhere at any time. All they will need is an interest, a pair of binoculars and a birding book, and they can learn about birds that inhabit any region.

Bird Feeders and Bird Baths

A good starting point for birdwatching is a bird feeder, birdbath or birdhouse installed in your own backyard or on a windowsill. Be sure to look for installations that are squirrel-proof and safe for birds. Select areas in your yard close to bushes or trees so that birds can flee to safety when they feel threatened. Also decide what size of bird you want to attract. If you want to feed both small and large birds, install separate feeders a distance apart. That way smaller birds do not have to compete with larger, more intimidating birds for food. If you plan to install a feeder in your garden, be aware of the fact that birdseed can sprout when it falls onto the ground among your other garden plants. To avoid this, try using shelled seeds.

What to Feed the Birds		
Wild Birds	**Prefer to Eat**	**Will Eat**
Blackbirds	Cracked corn, suet	Millet, bread, nuts
Cardinals	Sunflower seeds	Suet, apples, fruit
Chickadees	Sunflower seeds	Suet, bread
Doves	Millet	Sunflower seeds, bread, nuts
Finches	Sunflower seeds	Millet, suet

Hummingbirds	Plant nectar, insects	Sugar water
Jays	Peanuts	Sunflower seed, suet
Juncos	Millet, sunflower seeds	Cracked corn, peanuts
Mockingbirds	Fruit, berries	Suet, sunflower sees, nuts
Orioles	Fruit, nectar	Suet, raisins
Pigeons	Millet	Sunflower seeds, bread
Purple martins	Mosquitoes, beetles	Insects
Robins	Suet, mealworms, berries	Bread, raisins, nuts
Sparrows	Millet, sunflower seeds	Bread crumbs
Titmice	Sunflower seeds	Suet, bread
Woodpeckers	Suet, sunflower seeds, fruit	Meat scraps
Wrens	Suet	Peanut butter, apples

If you are trying to attract birds to your yard by building feeders, you should also install a birdbath. A bath is both a source of drinking water and bathing water. However, do not place a birdbath close to feeders. Birds do not like to bathe where there is a lot of other bird activity around them.

Getting Started

You will need only a pair of binoculars and a good field guidebook to start your kids birdwatching. You do not have to spend a great deal of money to purchase binoculars for birdwatching. If at all possible, it is a good idea for each child to have his or her own binoculars so that they can compare notes while looking at a bird.

There are field guides aimed at children who are interested in learning about birds (see Resources at the end of this chapter). Look for guides that focus on birdwatching beginners. Encourage your kids to refer to these guides as they tour the backyard and neighborhood. You will want to purchase a field guide for your own region; some popular guides have separate editions for the eastern and western regions of the United States as well as editions that cover Canada.

Start in your own yard and ask your kids to take notes on what they see. For example, they can describe a bird–its color, distinguishing markings, size–and list what the bird is eating (fruit, insects or seeds), where it appears to live and how its song or call sounds. These are all clues that they can use to identify a bird in the field guide.

You may have to explain to the younger kids what they are seeing. Call your children's attention to the way a bird flies, what it eats, how it sounds and what it looks like. Young children will soon be able to name common birds in your region while older kids can investigate unusual birds and try to identify them in a bird book.

If you own a camera, or can purchase even a disposable one, have your kids take pictures of the birds they see. Later they can compare the snapshot to photographs in the field guide. They can also use the photos to construct their own personal backyard field guide. Each child can paste a photo into an empty album or notebook and then list his or her observations about the bird.

Beyond Your Own Backyard

Once your children become familiar with the guidebook and have identified the most common birds in your own yard, you may want to venture out into neighboring territory. Before you start, sit down with the kids and make a list of common birds in your region. Include those you have seen in your own yard but also list birds that are unfamiliar to you. Armed with your binocular(s) and a field guide, take a birdwatching walk to search for the birds on your list. You can even divide the kids into teams and turn the walk into a scavenger hunt. The team with the most finds on the list is the winner.

Developing a Hobby

If your kids show an interest in pursuing birdwatching, investigate local birdwatching clubs. Most members are genuinely interested in helping newcomers learn about birds. Bird club people also can give you sound advice about gear, good birding locations and reference guides. You and your kids can even become part of weekly or monthly birding hikes in your own area or nearby regions.

Caring for a Baby Bird

It is inevitable that your child will discover a baby bird on the ground away from its home. Your first impulse is to help the bird–maybe even adopt it as a summer project. Resist that urge.

Baby birds do much better when their parents care for them. And it is not uncommon for a very young bird to leave the nest before it can fly or forage for food. Part of the reason for this is the fact that the nest becomes hazardous for the young birds. Their constant cheeping for food alerts squirrels, predator birds like hawks and even climbing cats that their nest is nearby. So if threatened, they abandon the nest.

When this happens, the parents shoo the babies back into foliage or shrubbery to hide while the parents continue to feed and care for them. After a few weeks they will be able to find food on their own and to fly. By that time they are fully developed and ready to leave home.

So if you or your kids see an unattended baby bird out in the open, it is best to place it in nearby vegetation or foliage so that the parents can find it and continue to care for it. Carefully pick the bird up using a towel and holding it firmly so that it will not hurt itself struggling to escape. Put the bird in the nearest tree or shrub where the parents can easily find it. Watch from a distance and you will soon see the parents locate the baby and give it food. Explain to your kids that the baby bird is much better off with its parents than with adoptive parents.

Resources

Take a Backyard Bird Walk, (Stillwater Publishing, 2001).

This book, written for children ages 4 to 8, is designed to be carried by kids as they birdwatch in their own backyard. It features pictures of common birds and pages on which to take notes.

Stokes Field Guide Series, (Little, Brown and Company).

These guides are recommended for kids and beginners because they include birds that a beginner is likely to spot.

Bird Watching for Dummies, (Wiley, 1997).

This book is a good introduction to birdwatching with practical tips and guidelines to birding.

Peterson Field Guides, (Houghton-Mifflin Books).

These field guides cover a wide range of topics including birds of prey, backyard birds and bizarre birds, and are easy to use for beginners.

www.thayerbirding.com

This Website offers Thayer Birding Software, which includes birding CDs for each state of the United States. The CDs feature photos, songs, videos and quizzes about birds.

Starting a Stamp Collection

If you are looking for a hobby to introduce your kids to that is both ongoing yet ever-changing, then stamp collecting is a good choice. It is an activity that your kids can pursue throughout their lives and it provides a way to explore geography and history. Plus, stamp collecting need not be expensive–the kids can collect used stamps simply by looking in your own mailbox.

Beginning with the Basics

There are a few details you and your kids should talk about before beginning to collect stamps, particularly if your kids are interested in making stamp collecting a continuing hobby.

Stamps are classified by type, format, purpose and condition:

Type

Stamps come in three types: definitive, commemorative and special.

- Definitive stamps are basic stamps, usually described as small, plain and issued in specific denominations to pay for different postage rates. In the United States, definitive stamps often have pictures of deceased presidents and other famous people, although recently, definitive stamps have depicted the White House and the flag.
- Commemorative stamps honor historical events such as Christopher Columbus' discovery a of the New World. Some depict anniversaries of states or organizations. These stamps are usually larger than definitive ones and are issued in smaller quantities.
- Special stamps honor special occasions and are limited in number. The most common are the Love stamp (for wedding invitations and Valentine's Day cards) and the Christmas stamp.

Format

Stamps come in three formats: sheets, booklets and coils (also known as rolls).

Purpose

Stamps are issued for five postal purposes: regular, special delivery, air mail, parcel post and postage due.

Condition

Stamps attain three conditions: mint, unused and used.

- Mint condition defines an unused stamp in the same condition as when it was issued.
- Unused condition describes an unused stamp with disturbed glue on its back.
- Used condition characterizes a stamp that has been used to pay for delivery of mail as indicated by its postmark.

The value of a stamp depends on its condition, its scarcity and its demand. That is why you want to understand the criteria for types and conditions of stamps. If you think your kids will pursue stamp collecting as a serious hobby, you also need to tell them about demand. Basically, if a lot of collectors are interested in a rare stamp, then that stamp has a high value. You will learn that there are other criteria indicating demand, but this basic definition is a good starting point.

Getting Started

Knowing the fundamentals of stamp collecting, however, may not be necessary if you are introducing your kids to the fun and educational aspects of the hobby. Children from preschool age through the teen years can collect stamps without concerning themselves with the type, format, condition or value of stamps. Many kids like developing and maintaining collections just for the fun of it.

In these cases, the first question your kids may ask concerns the kinds of stamps to collect and where find them. In answering, consider the ages and interests of the kids. Many kids like to collect stamps from other countries just to see what they look like. This can be simple if you have friends or relatives sending mail to you from abroad. The kids can refine it further by collecting stamps only from specific countries where family and friends live. You can ask your correspondents to use different stamps, if possible, when sending you mail. This kind of stamp collecting is a great opportunity for you to encourage your kids to learn about the history and culture of other countries. Pull out an atlas and read about the countries that issue the stamps.

Other kids enjoy topical collections, such as animals, birds, space or sports. Your kids may want to specialize even further by collecting only Olympic sports stamps or stamps commemorating black history. If your kids are very young, they can build a collection of stamps of a certain shape or color. You can tie this in with activities that teach about shape or color. If the kids have no preferences about the type of collection they want, they can simply collect any stamp that catches their eye and then save the collection in a safe place. After a while you the kids may see an interest or theme emerging, and they can then tailor their collection to reflect that interest.

Finding Stamps

All beginning stamp collectors need to gather stamps. Here are some sources of stamps for your kids' collections:

Your Own Mailbox

Give the kids an opportunity to look through your mail. Tell them that even metered mail or envelopes with bulk postage stamps can become collectible if they are sent from an interesting place.

Friends, Relatives and Neighbors

Have the kids ask everyone you know to save stamped envelopes for you. Most people throw away the envelopes and will happily save them for a budding collector.

Office or Business Mail

If a family member or friend works in an office, ask for envelopes from the office mail. Many companies receive mail from foreign countries. Or the kids can approach travel agencies, foreign government offices in the area or other companies that do business out of the country.

Old Letters

Search for old family letters or mementos that may have old or foreign stamps. Save the entire envelope until you know how valuable the stamp is. You do not want to remove a stamp from an envelope until you know if the stamp is worth more if it is still attached to the envelope.

Pen Pal

Suggest that your older children begin a pen pal correspondence with someone in another country. This will become more than just a good source of stamps; this is a way to make a new friend. Visit Student Letter Exchange *(www.pen-pal.com)* or World Pen Pals *(www.world-pen-pals.com)* to learn how to become a pen pal.

Stamp Club

Investigate schools, churches, YMCAs or local community centers to locate a stamp club for kids. If there is no such group in your community, suggest to your kids that they form their own club. They can ask at school if there are other beginning stamp collectors who would like to meet to learn about stamps and trade them.

Post Office or Stamp Dealers

Your kids can buy stamps from the post office if they need one or two in order to complete a collection. Or they can go to stamp dealers. Most beginners, however, need guidance when buying stamps from dealers since prices will vary, depending on condition and value. Ask your postmaster about stamp clubs or go to the telephone directory listings under the subject heading Stamps for Collectors. Your postmaster may also be able to tell you about any local stamp shows.

Using Stamp Tools

There are a few basic tools your kids will need as beginning collectors in order to maintain a stamp collection. Fortunately, they are inexpensive:

- An album to sort and display the stamps. You can make your own or buy one from a stamp dealer. Either way, you want to use acid-free paper. Do not use a photo album with sticky pages; these will damage your stamps.
- Hinges or mounts that are small folded pieces of paper or plastic sleeves with special glue on one side. You place your stamps inside the hinges or mounts rather than directly onto the album page.
- Tongs that are special tweezers with a gripping surface to handle stamps without damaging them. Oil and perspiration from your bare fingers can damage stamps.
- A magnifying glass to help you see the details on a small stamp.

If your kids show an interest in pursuing stamp collecting, they may want to buy a perforation gauge, a special tool to count the holes between stamps where you separate them. In addition, a watermark detector is helpful to find watermark designs that make it difficult to counterfeit a stamp. Knowing these details about a stamp helps the collector determine its value. A stamp catalog that contains illustrations to help identify and learn about stamps is also useful, but you can usually find one of these at the library. Nevertheless, this is a good birthday gift for the budding stamp collector.

Resources

www.stamps.org

This is the official Website of the American Philatelic Society.

www.bumperland.com/next.html

This Website describes how to put a collection together, including instructions about removing stamps from an envelope.

www.bumperland.com/album.html

This Website provides detailed suggestions for constructing a stamp album.

www.stamps.org/kids/January/stamps_tips.htm

This Website tells beginners how to soak stamps off and sort and mount them.

www.bnaps.org/stamps4kids/tradepre.htm

This Website from the British North American Philatelic Society offers tips on trading stamps and using a stamp catalog to place value on stamps.

www.glassinesurfer.com

This Website discusses stamp collecting for beginners and includes tips as well as information about stamp catalogs and books.

Building a
Family Tree

Creating a family tree is one activity that will interest children of all ages. Even very young children are fascinated by the relationships within their family, especially those relationships that affect them directly. Your 2-year-old is just beginning to sort out family members and figure out how grandma fits into the mommy-daddy-me family configuration. Older children may wonder about cousins or great-uncles, and children of all ages who are part of a blended family are interested in learning who fits where in which family.

Getting Started

There are several ways to begin to build the family tree. The approach you choose will probably depend on your kids' ages and level of interest.

Preschoolers

Very young children will begin any family tree with themselves, so that is where you should tell them to begin. The simple apple tree template is probably all they need or want to know at this age.

Ask the kids to draw and cut out apple shapes from red construction paper. Be sure each apple is large enough to accommodate a small photo. To make the tree, cut out a tree canopy shape from green construction paper and glue it to a large sheet of white paper or cardboard. If your family is large, you may want to sketch an outline of a tree on a large sheet of paper and have the kids color it green. Ask the kids to draw in the tree trunk with a brown marker or crayon.

Glue a photo to the center of each apple and then glue the apples to the tree. Have the child glue his or her apple to the top of the tree alongside any brothers and sisters. The next row should be the photos of the parents, and the bottom row should include the grandparents. Have the kids color in branches connecting the apples. The final result may be enough to satisfy your preschoolers' curiosity.

If your kids do want more information, ask them to interview family members and then develop a fact sheet for each one. You or your older children can write down the answers and help fill in the fact sheets. When you are finished, help the kids construct a family tree booklet, using the apple tree montage as the cover.

Older Children

If your older children help the young ones prepare their booklet, they may develop an interest in digging more deeply into the family's history. Be advised that once someone begins to delve into family history, there is a possibility of becoming totally absorbed in the search.

Older kids can start creating a more detailed family tree by interviewing family members on each branch of the tree. This includes grandparents, aunts, uncles, cousins and in-laws. Grandparents and older relatives love being asked for an appointment to be interviewed by a child in the family. For the sake of consistency and completeness, the kids should use a questionnaire that you help finalize. They can write in the answers during face-to-face interviews, or they can ask family members who live far away to fill out the questionnaire and return it. Computer-literate kids can even format the questionnaire on screen and ask the respondents to fill in their answers on screen as well.

It is a good idea to compose many questions before you start an interview. Some questions may not apply to everyone you talk with, but you do not want to forget to ask an important question. In addition to questions, prepare a list of items that may help build the family tree but that may not occur to those being interviewed. For example, ask your relatives if they have baby books, diaries, family bibles, invitations and announcements, certificates or diplomas, old letters, photo albums, scrapbooks, ID cards, trophies or awards and any family jewelry or furniture. Ask if you can see legal papers, deeds or wills. If some of the material is valuable or one-of-a-kind, offer to photocopy or digitally scan the items to preserve them. That way, the owner will be able to keep the original and there will be a backup copy as well.

Here is a sample questionnaire.

Questions for Family Interviews
1. What is your full name? What is your nickname?
2. What are your parents' full names?   What are your grandparents' full names?
3. Were you named after anyone?
4. When were you born? (provide month, day and year)

5. Where were you born? (provide town, county, state and country)

6. Do you have any brothers or sisters? (provide names and ages)

7. Where were each of your brothers and sisters born?

8. What are your favorite memories of each brother or sister?

9. What was your childhood home like? (provide details about their house, neighborhood, school and town)

10. What are your favorite memories of your home?

11. Was anyone in your family famous?

12. Was anyone in your family in trouble?

13. How did your family earn a living during your childhood?

14. How did you earn a living as an adult?

15. Did you like your job?

For immigrants:

16. What are your memories of your home before you came to this country?

17. Why did your family decide to emigrate?

18. How did your family earn a living in the old country?

19. What are your first memories after you arrived here?

20. What languages do you speak?

These are only sample questions to start the interviews. With your help, your kids can develop a more detailed list of questions tailored to your specific family.

When the kids have finished their questionnaires, they can use the information to learn more about the family background. The Internet is the ideal place to start. Refer to the Resources at the end of this chapter for Websites to begin the search.

The first and simplest task of your Internet search is to type your surname into a search engine. You may be amazed to discover how much information you can find on a simple search of your name. Visiting national census archives, the U.S. Social Security Death Index, cemetery records and newspaper obituaries online can also reveal a great deal of information. Go to the library and ask the librarian to help you find government and national archives. And do not forget to check the family bible, since it used to be the primary depository of family records and history.

Genealogical Fun for the Entire Family

After you have designed a family tree and discovered fascinating tidbits of family history, you and the kids can set up some family activities that are fun for all ages.

Plan a family history tour of neighborhoods where parents and grandparents grew up. Visit their homes, schools and even graveyards where the kids can make gravestone rubbings (first ask permission at the cemetery office). If you live near a neighborhood or site where immigrants entered the United States (such as Ellis Island in New York) or where your ancestors arrived, visit the area and take photos. When you return home, look at an atlas and try to plot the route your immigrant ancestors took to arrive in this country. Calculate the timeline for everyone in the family to emigrate to their new home. Look up facts about your family's countries of origin—what are the countries' languages, food specialties and music? Search out ways to make your family's history fresh and meaningful to everyone in the family.

Resources

My Family Tree Workbook, (Dover Publications, 1982).

This easy-to-use introduction to genealogy is especially geared toward children.

The Kids' Family Tree Book, (Sterling, 2007).

This book discusses ways that children can create a family tree.

Me and My Family Tree, (Dragonfly Books, 2000).

This is a story of a young girl's construction of her family tree. Written in simple and easy-to-understand language, the book explores two generations.

Family Tree Page Ideas for Scrapbookers: 130 ways to create a scrapbook legacy, (Memory Makers Books, 2004).

This book teaches scrapbookers how to create family tree pages and offers genealogical research tips and reproducible charts.

www.myfamily.com

This Website provides instructions on how to create your own family tree Website and includes tips on using photos, posting news and maintaining a chat room.

http://gov-records.com

This Website lists government records that allow online background checks into documents such as birth certificates, marriage certificates, adoption records and obituaries.

www.familysearch.org

This Website provides free family history and genealogy records.

Announcing a spontaneous picnic is a wonderful way to shake off the midsummer doldrums and generate a change of pace. Because it is impulsive, it does not require a lot of planning. Enlist the kids' help and ask what they want to do. You can substitute a picnic for breakfast, lunch or dinner, and if the weather spoils your plans, you can bring the picnic indoors. Sometimes picnicking on a blanket in the living room is more fun than fighting off mosquitoes outside.

Planning a Picnic

Even a last-minute idea, however, needs some planning. This is your chance to let the kids do the organizing themselves, particularly if you are picnicking in your own yard. Ask them to plan the picnic as if they were going to be somewhere other than their yard. This means that you should encourage them to pack everything they will need so that no one has to return to the house for anything. You can give them tips as they work: For example, be sure to include something to serve the food on and include utensils to dip into condiments. Mention sunscreen and insect repellent and remind them to designate a place to apply repellent that is far enough from food and eating areas.

If you decide to go to a park or picnic grounds away from home, you may have to supervise the packing more closely. Plus, you will want to show the kids how to pack food, utensils and other picnic items so that they do not spill, break or spoil. If you have a picnic basket outfitted with compartments and slots, help the kids pack that. If you do not have a basket, find a sturdy box, preferably with handholds, in which to pack and carry the goods. You will also need a cooler to keep food fresh and drinks cold. An inexpensive Styrofoam™ one will do. If you do not have a cooler, you can pack perishables in heavy plastic bags and place them in a waterproof box surrounded by bags of ice cubes. You can also use some of the ice cubes for your drinks at the picnic.

Here is a list of picnic staples you may want to keep in a corner of your pantry for picnic days:

- Picnic basket or carton
- Cooler
- Large blanket or tablecloth
- Towelettes, baby wipes or waterless soap
- Biodegradable paper plates and cups
- Recyclable flatware
- Plastic bags for ice and food
- Large plastic bag for trash and garbage
- Insect repellent
- Sunscreen
- First aid kit
- Charcoal, lighter and grill utensils

Food

What the kids want to eat will also determine how you plan your picnic. If they want to plan a menu around a grill, either in the backyard or at a park, you will need to pack food to be cooked. Do not forget tongs, spatulas and other grilling utensils. If you are going to a park that provides built-in grills, remember to take charcoal and lighter fluid. The cooking fire will be your responsibility unless you have a teen or older child who knows the safety rules for lighting a fire.

If the picnic is truly a spontaneous, last-minute idea, you will probably want to plan to bring cold food. Search your refrigerator and pantry for picnic foods. Be inventive. If you do not have enough bread to make sandwiches for everyone, take along tortillas, buns or biscuits. Let the kids create their own sandwiches with what you have at hand. Serve a hot dog in a tortilla or ham and cheese on a hotdog bun. Try peanut butter and sliced bananas on a biscuit. Or make cracker sandwiches. They crumble when you bite into them, but if you are outdoors, the wildlife will welcome the crumbs.

Here is a list of nonperishable food items you can keep on hand for picnic days:

- Juice boxes
- Raisins
- Nuts and/or trail mix
- Marshmallows
- Prepackaged cookies or graham crackers
- Chocolate bars
- Condiments (Save the packages of catsup, mustard, mayonnaise, salt and pepper from restaurants and carry-out food establishments.)

Add whatever fresh foods you find in your refrigerator, and you are ready for a picnic.

Picnic Recipes

There are a few standby recipes that have been a part of picnics for generations. You and the kids can either prepare these foods at home or take along the ingredients for everyone to make his or her own version at the picnic.

Ants on a Log

Ingredients:
> Celery stalks, washed and trimmed
> Peanut butter
> Raisins

Directions:
> Spread peanut butter into celery stalk cavity. Press raisins into peanut butter.

S'mores (Requires a Fire or Heat Source)

Ingredients:
> Chocolate bars that can be separated into squares
> Graham crackers
> Marshmallows

Directions:
> Toast marshmallows on a skewer or stick over a fire or a grill. Slip the marshmallow off the skewer onto chocolate squares arranged on a graham cracker. Top with another graham cracker to make a warm, melted sandwich.

> Note: the marshmallows must be fairly hot to melt the chocolate so you may need to supervise and help the younger kids make this recipe.

Spider Crackers

Ingredients:
> Round crackers
> Cream cheese, softened
> Small pretzel sticks
> Raisins

Directions:
> Spread cream cheese onto a cracker and press four pretzel sticks into the cream cheese so that the pretzels are equally spaced apart and stick out over the edge of the cracker. These are the spider's legs. Place raisins on the top of the cracker for eyes, using cream cheese to hold them in place.

Mud Pies

Ingredients:
  Pudding
  Chocolate sandwich cookies, crushed
  Chocolate chips
  Gummy worms

Directions:
  Mix together the cookies, chocolate chips and pudding. Garnish with gummy worms on top.

A picnic is a welcome diversion for kids of all ages. Encourage the older children to plan the picnic and carry out the work. You will be teaching organization and planning skills, especially if they take responsibility for the consequences when mistakes or omissions occur. Most kids will not forget the grilling utensils more than once.

For younger children, you can take along games and toys. Bubbles and wands are always welcome as are sidewalk chalk, balls and Frisbees®. If you are picnicking away from home, do not forget that babies and some toddlers need naps, so plan to bring along a stroller or infant swing for naptime. Some families even take the blanket or tablecloth used on the ground to fashion a sturdy sling to hang from a low branch of a tree for their babies to nap in. Meanwhile, the other kids can play or read nearby. Be certain, however, that everyone is awake and available for cleanup and packing when the picnic is over.

Resources

http://pbskids.org/arthur/parentsteachers/activities/acts/pretend_picnic.html

  This Website instructs parents how to assemble a pretend picnic as a beginning exercise for planning a real one.

http://stepbystepcc.com/picnic.html

  This Website includes songs, stories, games, arts and crafts, and themes appropriate for picnics.

www.growingkids.co.uk/Picnics.html

  This Website describes how to pack a great picnic and includes menus and recipes.

www.picnicportal.com

  This Website contains a collection of articles about picnics and picnic planning, including games, recipes and a picnic products buyers' guide.

Exercise Day

Exercise day is every day! Or to put it another way: Every day should be an exercise day. This is the message you want to instill in your children from the very beginning. Actually, imparting that message should not be too difficult since kids exercise all the time without even knowing it. Running during play, riding bikes, playing ball and climbing on playground equipment are good ways to build strong, healthy bodies. Problems arise when kids spend long periods of time in front of a computer or TV screen. It is during those sedentary times that you have to declare an exercise day to get them back into the habit of daily physical activity.

What Kids Need

Just what kind of exercise and how much of it do kids need? Health experts suggest that active children are more likely to be fit and that fitness includes endurance, strength and flexibility.

Endurance develops when kids engage in activities that makes their hearts beat faster and their lungs work harder; this is known as aerobic (air) exercise. Walking, running, skating and swimming build endurance. Climbing, wrestling and pushups build strength by working and toning muscles. Stretching exercises such as doing splits or flips improve flexibility. Making a point to set aside time for vigorous play every day will help ensure that your kids will become fit and remain so.

But how much vigorous play is necessary? According to the 2005 guidelines from the U.S. Department of Agriculture Pyramid Plan, all kids 2 years and older should participate in 60 minutes of active exercise every day. The American Heart Association also recommends 60 minutes of exercise each day consisting of 30 minutes of moderate activities and 30 minutes of vigorous exercise. In addition, the National Association for Sport and Physical Education (NASPE) recommends the following:

Age	Minimum Daily Exercise	Comments
Infant	No requirements	Encourage motor skills development
Toddler (1 to 2 years old)	1½ hours	30 minutes planned activity and 60 minutes free play
Preschooler (3 to 5 years old)	2 hours	60 minutes planned activity and 60 minutes free play
School age	1 or more hours	Can break up into 15-minute segments

Using these recommendations as guidelines, you should be able to formulate an exercise program for your kids. Bear in mind that your children do not have to meet the time recommendations in one chunk of time; you can suggest that they play or exercise several times each day. Remember, too, to take safety into account. Not all exercise and games are safe for all ages. Be sure each child's activities are suitable for his or her age, size and physical abilities. Also, check with your children's doctor about the types of exercise that are appropriate and healthy for your kids, especially those kids with chronic illnesses (asthma, for example) or disabilities.

Set a Good Example

You cannot expect your kids to be active unless you are active yourself. Let them see you live an active life-style. Take the stairs rather than the elevator, walk rather than drive, park on the far side of a parking lot, practice yoga and perform stretching exercises. Emphasize to your kids that the benefit of physical activity is the chance to take care of their body rather than a chore to be finished.

Make a competitive game of exercise. Carry a small notebook and jot down every time you substitute a physical activity for a sedentary one. Ask the kids if they can match your efforts in a day's time. Be sure to point out that they have the competitive edge, since much of their play is physical activity.

Establishing Exercise Day

You can reach some of the goals for your kids and yourself by designating a day devoted to exercise and physical activity. Let your kids choose the activities and set the pace. For example, if you have a child who likes to read, ride your bikes to the library. Encourage children who are interested in science to take a nature walk or hike. Your budding artists, too, can take walks to find materials for their craft projects or collages. Urge the kids to explore and climb during these walks. If you encounter resistance to abandoning the TV, pop in dance or exercise videos and guide the kids in following along with the videos.

Be sure to allow for a change of pace now and then. If the kids begin to lose interest, have a contest to see who can climb like a monkey, walk like an elephant, run like a panther or hop like a bunny. Younger kids enjoy this kind of activity. You can entice older kids to join in games, especially if you play with them. Try red rover, tag or relay races. Show the kids your talents at jumping rope–they may be quite surprised to hear you rattle off jump-rope chants. Or teach them the yoga movements you learned in a class or from a video.

Why not finish off some chores while exercising? Ask who can pull the most weeds in a given time period. Challenge a child to sweep out the garage with a push broom in fewer than 10 minutes. Time someone to run to the nearest mailbox with your important letters. Remind the kids that the dog needs to be walked and exercised and select someone to take on that duty. Kids are usually eager to help, especially when there is a time limit and the chore is a fun one to carry out rather than an endless and boring one.

Transforming Exercise Day into Exercise Everyday

Exercise day is not enough, however. Based on the suggested activity requirements for kids, you can see that one exercise day every now and then is not sufficient. You need to use the impetus and enthusiasm from the first exercise day to set up a daily routine that makes exercise a habit. This goal can be furthered by scheduling an exercise day on a regular basis–maybe once a month. If you are successful in making exercise a daily habit, your kids will show increased fitness, strength and endurance on each exercise day. This is a good way to evaluate each child's fitness progress.

How can you encourage your kids to make exercise a daily routine? First, of course, you need to be a role model. Second, you may need to limit computer and TV time. And third, you need to provide encouragement and equipment that makes exercise fun and spontaneous. For example, start with an inexpensive pedometer for each child. The kids will be curious–maybe even astounded–to learn how many steps they take each day. Wear one yourself to see just what kind of role model you are.

When it is birthday or holiday gift time, consider bicycles, skates, in-line skates or scooters. (Do not forget the appropriate safety gear.) Balls of all kinds, jump ropes, Hula Hoops® or pogo sticks promote active play. For rainy days or sweltering ones, look for activity or dance videos or indoor games like Twister.

If you have a yard or play area, set up equipment or games on a semi-permanent basis. For example, a regulation basketball hoop is always inviting for older kids. Or keep a volleyball or badminton net set up in the backyard. If you have room, place a bin for sports gear in the garage or on a porch. The kids can keep balls, ball mitts, ball bats (supply wiffle balls and bats for young children), jump ropes, badminton rackets and birdies, in-line skates and other sports equipment readily available for use. And the bin makes it easy for you to toss equipment in the car for a trip to the park.

What about finding time for daily activity? If your household is busy, you may have to allot time for it. Perhaps you can send your kids out to play or run for half an hour while you prepare dinner, as mothers and grandmothers have done for generations. Late morning may better suit your family's schedule or you may prefer after dinner when it is cooler. Try to avoid vigorous exercise right before bedtime; otherwise, your kids may not be able to settle down to sleep.

Resources

www.mypyramid.gov

This is the official Website of the U. S. Department of Agriculture's Health Pyramid. This site recommends dietary and exercise guidelines for optimal health for all ages.

www.americanheart.org

This is the Website for the American Heart Association, which provides information to parents and kids about heart health and heart exercise.

www.fitnessandkids.com

This Website presents health, exercise and fitness equipment for kids.

www.eyelearner.com

This Website lists children's fitness videos that help children become fit and prevent obesity.

41

Learning a
New Sport

Most kids are naturally active. Vigorous play is an integral part of childhood, and children often get enough exercise without even knowing it. If you encourage exercise and active play and if you set a good example by showing your kids how to live an active life-style, your kids should be fit and healthy.

You can go a step further, however. As kids become adults, they begin to relinquish the games and play of their childhood and become more sedentary. But you can help offset this natural progression by encouraging your kids to learn and practice what are known as life sports. These are the activities that they can pursue throughout their lives and the best time to learn these skills is in childhood.

Life sports include activities such as swimming, cycling, tennis, gymnastics, golf and dance. Some adults also enjoy joining sports teams and leagues such as soccer, baseball, softball and bowling. Hiking and walking are also popular pastimes.

How Young Can a Child Start?

Older toddlers and preschoolers can play some sports if you can find a program that is noncompetitive and geared toward teaching basic rules of a game or sport. If you think your younger kids are ready to learn a sport, particularly a team sport, check out the YMCA, local parks and recreation programs or city leagues. Many of these organizations offer programs for young kids that teach the basics of a game and team play but do not keep score. There may be tot soccer games, T-ball and gymnastics; also, there may be aquatics classes that introduce the kids to water fun and swimming. Ask to sit in on a class or a practice to see if the activities fit your kids' needs and abilities. Even more important, however, is to determine how carefully the kids are supervised. Remember that at this early age, your kids are not ready for contact sports or heavy competitiveness. Rather, you want a program that promotes coordination, cooperation, active play and fun.

As the kids reach preschool age, typically between 3 or 4 to 5 years of age, they can expand their horizons a little. Although there are gymnastics programs for kids at any age–even classes for infants and toddlers–gymnastics classes grow progressively more physically demanding as kids grow older. This is an example of a sport that can grow as the kids grow, provided, of course, that your kids want to continue participating. Many other sports programs also become a little more formal for kids from the age of 4 years and older. The American Academy of Pediatrics recommends that parents wait until their kids are 4 years old before enrolling them in programs for T-ball, flag football, soccer or formal swimming lessons, since by that age, you may be able to recognize which sports appeal to your kids. Again, however, ask to watch a practice or class before enrolling your kids to see if the children are well supervised and if the activities fit the kids' needs. In addition, determine the teacher or coach's attitude toward sportsmanship. Learning to be a good winner or loser is as important as learning how to be a good player.

Team Versus Individual Sports

After all of your research into sports programs for your kids, you learn that one or more of the kids either are not ready or do not like team sports. This is normal– not all 3- to 5-year-olds are ready for team sports. In fact, even many older kids and adults do not enjoy them. If you find yourself in this situation, how can you help your kids develop lifelong exercise habits?

The answer is to encourage your kids to take up an individual sport, one that does not have the pressure of working within a team but that does encourage your child to compete with him- or herself to improve skills, fitness and stamina. Swimming, bicycling, running, dancing, weightlifting, golf, bowling, canoeing, tennis and water skiing are just a few of the sports that kids and adults can pursue on their own. What about something different like orienteering that teaches map reading and mapmaking while hiking in wilderness areas? Some require money, equipment and facilities (cycling, weightlifting, tennis, swimming or bowling) while others require only determination and time (running or dancing). In the interest of health and fitness, you should encourage individual pursuits even if you have to make a financial investment in equipment. If you are unsure about your child's long-term commitment to a new sport, borrow equipment or buy it secondhand. Look for garage sales or post a notice on the grocery store bulletin board. It may turn out that buying equipment is less expensive than paying registration fees for a sports team that your child will not enjoy.

One warning about individual sports: Do not allow your kids to become obsessive about training. This is supposed to be fun, not a compulsory or compulsive activity.

And make sure that your kids stretch before and after exercise, drink plenty of water and inform you of any aches, pains or injuries after exercising.

Contact Sports

As your kids grow older, they may ask to participate in contact sports such as football, soccer, volleyball or basketball. There are both advantages and disadvantages to contact sports. Advantages include the opportunity to:

- Learn a new sport;
- develop sportsmanship;
- understand how to work as a team;
- experience the joy of working as part of a team;
- make new friends;
- exercise self-discipline through training;
- learn how to accept criticism and praise; and
- develop a healthy habit for life.

Disadvantages include the possibility of developing:

- An injury;
- an obsessive competitiveness; or
- a commitment to a sport that is inappropriate for the child.

If you think you child's temperament is suited to a competitive contact sport, investigate with your child the particular sport she wants to play. Remember that kids are not little adults. They are still growing with developing bones, muscles, tendons and ligaments. Growth plate injuries are common and can be serious. The growth plates, areas of cartilage where bone growth occurs, are weaker than adjacent ligaments and tendons and thus are especially susceptible to injury. A simple bruise in an adult may be a serious growth plate injury in a child. While these injuries can occur during any type of exercise, they are more likely to be a result of vigorous contact sports.

You can avoid problems by taking a few precautions. First, take your children to the doctor for a thorough physical checkup and ask the doctor to advise the kids about safety when playing a contact sport. Second, select the proper safety gear for each child. Be sure it is the right size and fits well. Emphasize to your kids that they listen to their body. If they experience pain, they should stop playing. Kids should never walk off pain by continuing to play a game.

When you look into summer sports programs, choose a program that places children on teams according to size, weight and ability rather than age. Children of the same age–especially preteen kids–may differ widely in size and skills. And the smaller child is at a disadvantage when playing with or against larger, stronger children.

Ask to speak with the coaches. If a coach emphasizes winning rather than having fun or sportsmanship, then this is the wrong program for your child. Look at the playing area and the equipment. Are both in good condition and is there enough safety gear for every team member?

Finally, while you are investigating the program, review the schedule. Will practice times and games fit into your schedule? Because this is a summer program, you may be tempted to be casual about missing practices but a child who has not practiced is more vulnerable to injury.

A Handicapped Game

Occasionally, you may find your home full of kids of different ages who are bored and looking for something to do. This could be a chance to teach a new way to play a sport–the handicapped game.

Assemble all the kids and form two baseball teams. Explain the basic rules of baseball (for the benefit of the preschoolers) and then ask the kids to figure a way they could all play baseball together. If they are stumped, explain handicapping.

For example, every child under age 4, or under a certain height, would get five strikes. Kids 10 years and older would get two strikes and the others in between would get the usual three strikes. A child too young or small to run fast could be designated as a pinch runner. Outfielders could move in when a preschooler batted and out when a preteen batted. A hit beyond second base would be a home run for a preschooler. And so on, until you achieve a balance that allows the teams to play an almost normal game. Let the kids figure out the handicaps–you may be amazed at how well they can set up this game. Everyone plays and there is a feeling of cooperation and sportsmanship. Plus, you did not have to drive the group to practice or think up several activities for the different ages of the kids.

Resources

www.aap.org/healthtopics/sports.cfm

This Website of the American Academy of Pediatrics offers tips for parents who are investigating sports for their children.

www.growingkids.co.uk/TeamGames.html

This Website offers advice about children playing team games. The site also has pages about contact sports and athletics for kids.

A New Cookie
Each Week

Looking for a new cookie recipe each week during the summer and then trying it out can be a fun activity. This is one way for the kids to practice measuring and cooking techniques as they help prepare meals with the family (see Chapter 1, *Learning to Cook*). Plus, you and the kids will keep the family in homemade snacks and desserts all summer long.

There is one drawback, however. Do you really want to turn on an oven on a hot day? Does baking sound like fun when it is 90 degrees outside? Do you want to put an extra strain on your air conditioning system just to bake a batch of cookies?

There is an answer. No-bake cookies. Not only do no-bake cookies eliminate the need to fire up the oven, they are also easy for kids to make. Some recipes need a little stovetop cooking, but many no-bake cookies require no cooking at all, which makes them ideal for young kids who are not yet ready to master the stove and oven.

For the sake of variety, you might want to introduce the kids to icebox cookies, named after the old-fashioned refrigerator that cooled its contents with blocks of ice rather than with electricity. To make icebox cookies, you mix a cookie dough and then roll the uncooked dough into a log or cylindrical block. Place the dough in the refrigerator for about 12 hours; this allows enough time for the dough to stiffen so that you can cut it into thin rounds or squares to form cookies. Most icebox recipes can also be stored in the freezer, ready to bake into fresh cookies whenever needed. The advantage to this kind of cookie is that they can be baked at any time, even from the freezer, so whenever you have a cool day, you have ready-to-bake dough to turn into warm cookies.

Finally, no matter what kind of climate you have, you and the kids will probably bake a few of the old standby recipes during the summer. Who can resist chocolate chip, oatmeal, peanut butter or sugar cookies? If you are in the mood to experiment, try something different by looking for variations of standard recipes.

No-Bake Cookies

Here are a few no-bake cookie recipes, starting with some simple ones and progressing to those that are slightly more complex.

Peanut Butter Balls with Crispy Rice Cereal

Ingredients:
 ½ cup peanut butter
 ¼ cup honey
 ½ teaspoon vanilla
 2 to 3 cups crispy rice cereal

Directions:
 Combine peanut butter, honey and vanilla. Stir in enough cereal to form balls (moisten hands first). Place balls on waxed paper and chill.

Orange Sticks

Ingredients:
 3½ cups vanilla wafer crumbs
 1 16-ounce box confectioners' sugar
 1½ cups pecans, chopped
 1 6-ounce can orange juice concentrate, thawed and undiluted
 ½ cup butter, melted
 1 7-ounce package flaked coconut

Directions:
 Combine and mix vanilla wafer crumbs, sugar and pecans. Stir in orange juice concentrate and butter. Shape into two-inch sticks and roll in coconut. Refrigerate until firm. Makes 4 to 5 dozen.

Oatmeal Raisin No-Bake Cookies

Ingredients:
 ½ cup peanut butter
 ½ cup honey
 ¼ cup orange juice concentrate
 1½ cups powdered milk
 2 cups rolled oats
 1½ cups raisins

Directions:
 Combine and mix all ingredients thoroughly. Roll into balls and then flatten. Refrigerate. Makes 3 dozen.

Chocolate Chip Bars

Ingredients:

1 bag chocolate chip cookies
1 large container whipped topping
1 cup milk (or more as needed)
Chopped nuts, coconut or sprinkles

Directions:

Dip cookies in milk and layer in 9- x 13-inch pan. Spread two or three
layers of whipped topping over the cookies. Sprinkles with nuts, coconut or
sprinkles. Cover and refrigerate overnight. Cut into bars.

Chinese Noodle Cookies

Ingredients:

1 cup chocolate chips
¾ cup vanilla-flavored chips
1½ cups butterscotch-flavored chips
6½ cups Chinese noodles

Directions:

Place all the chips into the top of a double boiler over simmering water until
melted. You could also do this in a glass bowl in a microwave oven. Stir often.
Remove from heat and stir in Chinese noodles. Drop by spoonfuls onto waxed
paper on a cookie sheet. Refrigerate until firm.

Frozen Treats

Ingredients:

Chocolate chips
Mini-marshmallows
Whipped topping
Graham crackers

Directions:

Mix together the first three ingredients to taste. Use mixture to create
graham cracker sandwiches. Freeze. Or you can simply substitute ice
cream for the filling.

Do not forget the old standby, rice cereal treats. Check the cereal box for the
proper proportions of cereal to margarine or butter and mini-marshmallows. Melt
butter and marshmallows together, add cereal and press into a pan or mold. This
does not have to be chilled, just cooled.

Icebox Cookies

There are many recipes available for icebox cookies. You and the kids can make vanilla, chocolate, lemon, orange and other flavors to store in the refrigerator or freezer. You can easily have some variety by mixing vanilla cookies first and then dividing the dough into several parts, each part of which has a different flavor.

A good way to store icebox cookies is to pack the dough into an empty paper towel tube. This makes the cookies uniformly round and enables you to store the cookie tubes compactly in the refrigerator or freezer. Roll the dough into a cylinder about two inches in diameter. Cut the cardboard tube lengthwise and line the interior with waxed paper. Place the cylinder of cookie dough on the waxed paper, close the tube and secure the package with rubber bands. Label and place in the refrigerator or freezer. When you are ready to bake cookies, open the tube and, using a meat slicer or very sharp knife, slice the dough into one-inch c-shaped cookies. Or you can slide a piece of dental floss under the width of the cookie roll and cross both ends of the floss on top of the roll. Pull the ends of the floss together in order to pinch the dough into a round shape. Bake in a 400-degree oven for 8 to 10 minutes.

Old Standbys

When nothing else will do but an old favorite cookie recipe, dig out your favorites and put the kids to work. If you or the kids want something a little different, ask the kids to go through cookbooks or even online to find satisfactory substitutes for the old favorites. For example, instead of sugar cookies, try a batch of snicker doodles. Dress up chocolate chip cookies by adding dried cranberries or apricots. Instead of raisins in oatmeal cookies, use Spanish peanuts. Ask the kids for ideas. They may be more innovative than you expect, and together you could invent a new cookie recipe.

Resources

http://allrecipes.com/recipe/no-bake-cookies-i/detail.aspx

This Website offers no-bake cookie recipes.

www.recipegoldmine.com/cooknobake/cooknobake.html

This Website provides additional no-bake cookie recipes in varying degrees of complexity.

www.texascooking.com/features/july2003refrigeratorcookies.htm

This Website explains the background and uses of icebox cookies. There are also tips on storing and baking them.

Build a
Tree House

Where can you escape the earthbound problems of the world? Where can you find a retreat like a private bird's nest, where you could survey your domain? The answer, of course, is a tree house.

Tree houses have long been a symbol of freedom–for kids seeking freedom from adults or adulthood, or from duties or responsibilities. How can you possibly concern yourself with down-to-earth chores when you are partaking of the gravity-defying atmosphere in a tree? Part of the appeal of building a tree house is that it fulfills a parent's inspiration was well as a kid's. It is fun to plan a tree house, to research the best way to go about the task and to work together as a family to build it.

Building a tree house is not a small undertaking, however. Before you embark on such an ambitious project, you need to investigate what building a tree house actually entails.

Planning and Design

Before you even begin to make plans, you need to contact your town's local department of planning and building regulations. Most properties will have legal restrictions on what can be built. These requirements vary from area to area and may be especially restrictive in cities, towns and suburban areas. If you own land in a rural area, you may be less encumbered when it comes to building codes and regulations. But it is essential that find out ahead of time what you can and cannot do. You may learn that a tree house is out of the question, or you may discover that the regulations are lenient enough that you can plan some sort of tree house on your property.

Some of the restrictions you may face include height restrictions on the tree house; restrictions that are easy to exceed when you start building. You may be prevented from building within a specified distance from a boundary line; this will determine which tree you can select. There will also be requirements regarding water and electrical connections to the tree house.

Once you have cleared the local housing authority, however, you still want to contact your neighbors as a courtesy. You do not want neighbors to complain that your tree house is an eyesore or overhangs their property. If you do not extend the courtesy of discussing this with neighbors, you run the risk of facing a lawsuit, fines or demolition orders, not to mention ill-will and tension among neighbors.

Remember, too, you may have all ages of kids playing in the tree house, so you want to be certain that the house is safe, sturdy and accessible for kids of different abilities. This might be the time to look into liability issues if a child gets hurt because of the tree house.

If you think it is legal and feasible to build a tree house, you can start planning your structure. You may want to consult with the kids at this stage, or you may want to do enough planning to determine the cost and time needed to complete the project before you mention it to them. If the kids become involved, ask them what they envision a tree house to be. Be prepared to explain any legal, financial or time restrictions that their plans may involve. This is the time to make some sketches and gather enough ideas to determine what materials you will need. You also have to select a tree, and the kids will want to include their opinion in that discussion. Ask them, too, about any extra features they might like. For example, they may want to hang a rope swing from the supports, a rope and pulley system for hauling supplies into the tree house, a special kind of ladder or a hammock for naps. Make a list of everything you and the kids would like to see in a tree house and then sort the items into a must have list, a would-be-nice list and a blue-sky list. These lists will help you decide how to proceed from this point.

This may be the time for you and the kids to research how to build the tree house. Refer to the books in the Resources section at the end of this chapter to find out if you want to tackle this project yourself. On the other hand, it might be wiser to contact a tree house building company to visit your property in order to create a set of plans for your site. Try contacting TreeHouse Workshop (*www.treehouseworkshop.com*) for ideas. Ask about having someone visit your place to consult with you about your plans.

Choosing a Tree

Almost any healthy, mature tree, including oak, maple, beech, ash or cedar, is suitable for a tree house. However, you must consider location, height and size. A tree standing alone in the middle of a yard (to meet the legal boundary requirements), for example, may be more vulnerable to wind than one in a cluster of trees. Tree houses themselves catch wind, but the risk is lessened if the tree house is low in the tree and if it has open walls or windows that allow air to pass through.

The taller the tree and the higher you build, the better your sense of freedom, but you have to think about safety, wind pressures and the amount of support needed for the tree house. Most often a tree house for kids should be around 10 feet off the ground for safety reasons. And, contrary to logic, the tree house will not move higher as the tree grows. Trees grow by expanding their diameter and growing new branch tips; thus, a tree house attached to the heartwood of the tree will not move higher.

The thickness of the branches is also important, because the branches need to be thick and sturdy enough to support the weight of the house and its occupants as well as the attachments to hold the house in place. The usual recommended thickness of a branch for a one-story tree house is eight inches.

What about damage from bolts, nails and cables? As a rule, proper use of bolts, nails or screws or bolts will not hurt the tree–the attachments simply penetrate the bark and go into the dead wood inside. Cables and ropes, on the other hand, can damage bark as the structure moves. That is why specific instructions about attaching the tree house to the tree are critical to know before you start building. Because this affects the health of the tree and the safety of the tree house, most parents turn to professionals to help plan and construct the tree house.

Do-It-Yourself or Call in the Professionals?

Many parents enjoy working with their kids to build a tree house. And if you have carpentry skills and can follow plans designed for a tree house, you will enjoy the challenge. However, because of the specific requirements regarding trees, supports, appropriate building materials and other factors that pertain to tree houses, you may want to consult or even hire professionals to help you. Remember, you do not want to harm the tree, you want the structure to be safe and accessible and you want to customize the house to your specifications. Plus, you will need to waterproof and windproof the house and if you live in a temperate or cool climate, you will have to winterize the structure. For these reasons, you may want to rely on a builder who knows about the essentials of a tree house and thoroughly understands them.

Resources

www.barbarabutler.com

This is the Website of Barbara Butler, one of the better-known playhouse/tree house designers.

www.thetreehouseguide.com/plans.htm

This Website offers practical design information to help you build your own tree house. There is also a section on building advice to help you with the actual construction.

How to Build Treehouses, Huts & Forts, (Lyons Press, 2003).

This book contains fun projects that parents and kids can build together in their backyards. Beginning with a section on basic carpentry, this book provides step-by-step instructions on building tree houses, forts and huts.

Treehouses You Can Build, (Gibbs, Smith Publisher, 2006).

This book provides tree house building basics to help you plan your own unique tree house. Also included are interviews with 50 families who built tree houses.

The Treehouse Book, (Universe Publishing, 2000).

This book offers detailed plans and drawings of tree house structures. The authors also describe their tree house-discovery expedition across the United States in search of all types of tree houses.

Treehouses: The Art and Craft of Living Out on a Limb, (Houghton Mifflin, 1994).

This book provides a brief history of tree houses from ancient times to the Victorian Age. Additionally, the author tells the stories of specific tree houses and their builders, ranging from kids' playhouses to actual living quarters for adults.

Board
Games

Board games have been fun diversions for generations. You can probably remember whiling away a long afternoon with a board game such as Monopoly, Clue, or Scrabble™ when it was too hot or rainy to play outside. Today, the old standbys are still around, but there are also new board games–some that are based on TV shows and some occurring as byproducts of children's book series. Many can be played on the computer, but your kids may find that sitting down to a board game with other players is more fun.

Here are a few suggested board games, grouped by age.

Games for Young Kids (Age 6 and Under)

Zingo™

This preschool bingo-style game, using picture tiles, teaches shape and pattern recognition as well as short-term memory skills. Can be played by two to eight players. No reading required. Made by ThinkFun.

Chutes and Ladders

Children learn counting and number recognition as they travel along the game board to get to the top. Land on a good deed space and a ladder will race you ahead, but watch out for the chutes that can send you back down! Containing a game board, spinner with arrow, four pawns with stands and instructions, Chutes and Ladders is a classic game that can be played by two to four players. Made by Hasbro.

I Spy Memory Game

Developed from the popular *I Spy* book series published by Scholastic, this game requires the players to match an object on one page with an object hidden or cleverly disguised in the picture on the facing page. There are also fun memory riddles. Beginners search for matching pairs while advanced players solve the riddles. Containing 60 memory cards and 15 riddle cards, the game offers eight ways to play, and there can be one to six players. No reading required. Made by Briarpatch.

Briarpatch Thomas & Friends™ Tracks & Trestles Game

This game is a new railway adventure for Thomas the Train fans. The players ride the rails up and down, all over the Island of Sodor. The first trusty engine to reach the shed is the winner. This game promotes visual, matching and manual dexterity skills. Containing a game board, spinner, six Thomas & Friend character pawns, this game is designed for two to six players. No reading required. Made by Briarpatch.

Money Bingo Game

Money bingo is a learning game that builds addition skills using coins. Made by Educational Learning.

Food Pyramid Bingo® Game

Learning about good nutrition is important and can be fun with Food Pyramid Bingo. Based on the U.S. Department of Agriculture's Food Pyramid recommendations for nutrition and exercise, this game teaches the basics of good eating habits. Made by Educational Learning.

Cranium Cariboo

This Cranium game is great for young kids, who must match shapes, colors and more. Players have to match cards and open doors to discover whether there is a ball underneath. Collect six balls to get the treasure. Made by Cranium.

Sorry!

Sorry offers players the opportunity to use of a lot of strategy and luck to get their game pieces from the start field to the home field on the board. Players can send each others' pieces back to the start field. The uniqueness of this board game is that there is no dice; rather, players have to draw cards with numbers that allow certain actions. Made by Hasbro.

Twister

This all-time favorite classic is an excellent icebreaker! There is a mat with different-colored discs on which a player has to place a hand or a foot. Rotating the spinner gives instructions on what color disc is to be selected on the mat, as well as whether a hand or a foot has to be placed there. Made by Milton Bradley.

Connect Four

This classic kids' game for two players is similar to tic tac toe except that it is played vertically. The aim of the game is to get four checkers in a row first, while preventing your opponent from doing the same. Made by Milton Bradley.

Games for School-Age Kids (Ages 7 to 12)

I Spy Game—Word Scramble

One or more players scramble to spell words by sliding interlocking letter tiles into place before time runs out. Score points for every letter used. Containing game board, 48 sliding letters, sand timer and 26 double-sided *I Spy* cards. Made by Briarpatch.

Monopoly—SpongeBob SquarePants Edition

This game for two to six players will appeal to kids who love SpongeBob Squarepants. Containing a game board, title deed cards, money and banker's tray, six collectible tokens, one plankton coin, two dice, 16 life preserver cards, 16 treasure chest cards, 32 pineapple houses, 12 Krust Krab restaurants and instructions. Made by Hasbro.

Pictionary® Junior

Pictionary Junior, a game for three or more players, is the game in which players select a card and attempt to draw the word that is printed on the card so that their team can guess which word it is. In the kids' board game version, the words to be drawn are easier than those in the adult version. Containing a game board, one die, timer, 144 cards, two pencils, two playing pieces and a pad of paper. Made by Hasbro.

Trivial Pursuit® for Kids—Volume 6

Trivial Pursuit for Kids is a game filled with new topics and 1,200 multiple-choice questions. Players, from two to six or teams, choose from categories like music, movies and games. New multiple-choice questions increase the chances of answering questions correctly. This game has all the fun and challenge of the adult editions, with questions specifically written for kids. Containing a game board, 200 question-and-answer cards, six tokens, 36 scoring wedges, one six-sided die and instructions. Made by Hasbro.

Scrabble™

The classic bestselling board game Scrabble is familiar to everyone; basically the aim of the game is to make the most scoring words as possible, crossword style, from seven letter tiles on the Scrabble board. This board game for two to four players teaches children about vocabulary and spelling. Containing a game board, 100 letter tiles, four wooden tile racks and a letter bag. Made by Hasbro.

Battleship

Battleship, a classic favorite for kids and adults alike, is a game where skill and luck play an important part in determining naval strategy. The aim of the game is to conceal the location of your ships from your opponents, while attempting to figure out the location of your opponent's ships. Played by two people. Made by Milton Bradley.

Yahtzee™

Yahtzee is the game of dice. Five dice are thrown at the same time. A scoring card has to be filled out with the results with different combinations receiving different points. The most highly regarded combination of dice is five of a kind, or Yahtzee. Designed to be played by two to ten players. Made by Milton Bradley.

Clue

This mystery whodunit is addictive and enjoyable for the entire family. It is fun to figure out who has murdered the victim from the entire cast of characters and with which murder weapon. Containing a game board, six suspect tokens, six weapons tokens, deck of suspects, weapons and room cards, confidential case file, detective notebook pad, two dice and instructions in English and Spanish. This game can be played by three to six players. Made by Hasbro.

Boggle Jr.

This educational game for two to six players includes dice with alphabetical lettering on all six faces. The purpose of the game is to make as many words as you can from the letters that are currently displayed, within the three-minute time interval. Made by Parker Brothers.

Cranium Hullabaloo

This exciting game from Cranium comes in a box with a set of 16 little floor pads and a speaker unit. The pads, which have shapes, colors and pictures, are close enough to hop onto one from another. A voice from the speaker box gives instructions of various combinations of actions to take. After a few turns, a freeze command is called out and a winner is selected. Made by Cranium.

Resources

The following Websites provide information about various board games, including information about purchasing, playing or evaluating individual board games.

www.boardgames.com
www.hasbro.com
www.BoardGamesCatalog.com
www.TheToysCatalog.com
www.areyougame.com
www.educationallearninggames.com/educational-bingo-games.asp
http://store.cranium.com
http://boardgamecentral.com

Fourth of July Decorating

Falling in the middle of a long dry spell between Memorial Day and Labor Day, the Fourth of July is usually celebrated with much fanfare and excitement. After all, it is a festive holiday, commemorating the founding of the United States, and the seasonally temperate weather contributes to an enjoyable celebration.

The Fourth of July is a perfect opportunity for you to undertake a history lesson while you are planning your family's festivities. A week or so before the Fourth, before making your plans, organize a library day to gather information about the holiday. You will be proud later when you discover that your kids are among the few in the neighborhood who know why they are celebrating the Fourth of July.

As the holiday approaches, sit down with your kids to decide how you would like to spend the holiday. Many communities sponsor parades, which are good starting points for the day's festivities. Perhaps you would like to invite friends and family to a barbecue afterwards. If so, allow the kids to help plan the party, including the food, the games and, most of all, the decorations. Among the big decorating holidays, the Fourth of July ranks third behind Christmas and Halloween. Just think red, white and blue, and all sorts of ideas spring to mind.

Patriotic Pom-Poms

You can start by helping your kids construct patriotic pom-poms to take to the parade. You will need:

- several packs of 20- x 20-inch tissue paper in red, white and blue
- scissors
- rubber bands

For each pom-pom, stack 12 sheets of tissue paper, alternating red, white and blue. From one end of the pile, cut 40 ½-inch-wide strips, stopping about five inches from the other end of the stack. Roll up the cut strips loosely and then cinch the uncut end with a rubber band to form a handle. If you want, you can attach the pom-pom to a small dowel rod or stick. You are now ready to go to the parade.

There are three approaches you can when it comes to Fourth of July decorations: You can decorate your home, your cooking and yourself. Depending on how elaborate you want to be, you and the kids can have a lot of fun thinking of ways to carry out the patriotic theme.

Decorating Your Home

The stars, stripes, and colors of the American flag can be used to demonstrate your patriotism and creativity.

The American Flag

Many families display the American flag on national holidays, and what better day than the Fourth of July. If you do display the flag, you should be aware of proper flag etiquette, and, just as important, you should teach your kids the proper way to display it. Here are some rules for the respectful display of the flag:

- Display the flag only between sunrise and sunset unless it is illuminated in darkness, in which case you can display the flag 24 hours a day.
- Do not display the flag in bad weather.
- Do not allow the flag to touch the ground.
- Discard a flag that is tattered or faded by burning it.
- Fold the flag into a triangle when it is not on display (the triangle represents the tricorn hats worn by the colonial soldiers in the Revolutionary War).

String of Stars

In addition to the flag, your kids can craft other red, white and blue decorations for your home. For example, drape a decorative string of stars along a wall or intersperse with red, white and blue crepe streamers across the ceiling of your dining room or outdoor porch. To make the star string, you will need:

- construction paper (red, white and blue)
- cardboard
- scissors
- string or yarn (red, white or blue)
- stapler, tape or glue

Ask the kids to draw a large star on a piece of cardboard. If they want, they can look for a picture of a star to trace. Cut out the cardboard star to use as a template. Trace around the template on construction paper to make as many stars as you would like. Cut out the star and decorate it if desired. Fold over one tip of the star and staple, tape or glue it to a length of string. Continue making and adding stars until you have the length you need. Leave some extra string at the ends for hanging.

Red, White and Blue Wind Sock

A colorful wind sock on your front porch or on the corner of the house always looks festive. Gather together:

- a cylindrical cardboard oatmeal box
- construction paper (blue and white)
- red and white crepe paper streamers
- glue
- string
- scissors
- a hole punch

Cut the top and bottom off the oatmeal box, cover the box with blue construction paper and then glue on white construction paper stars. Cut some red and white crepe paper streamers and then glue or staple them to one end of the wind sock.

Punch four holes along the top rim of the wind sock. Cut two pieces of string about a foot long. Tie the strings to the wind sock through the punched holes (loop and knot the opposite ends of each string through the holes on the opposite sides of the cylinder). Tie a longer piece of string to the smaller pieces to hang the wind sock.

Patriotic Flower Pots

To add another decorative touch to your porch or yard, assign the kids the task of painting flower pots in patriotic colors. You will need unglazed terra cotta plant pots; red, white and blue acrylic paint and brushes. Have the kids paint the rim of the flowerpot white and the lower part of the pot blue (or vice versa). Allow the pot to dry and apply a second coat if needed. After the paint is completely dry, have the kids paints stars and stripes in contrasting colors on the pots. Look for a star template at craft stores so that the kids can simply stencil stars onto the pots.

When the pots are finished, plant some red and white flowers in them. Geraniums and white daisies look nice and can withstand small hands planting them.

Decorating for a Patriotic Party

Planning a barbecue party with a Fourth of July theme can be fun. Because the holiday falls within the growing season, food decorating can also be easy.

Let the kids help in the planning and the work. They can construct handmade invitations and suggest menu items. The simplest menu is one that is all-American—hot dogs, hamburgers, potato salad, corn on the cob and apple pie. However, your table will look especially patriotic if you lay out some red, white and blue food. For example, bake a simple yellow sheet cake in a 9- x 13-inch pan. When it has cooled, prepare some buttercreme frosting and divide the batch into three parts. Set one part aside for the white stripes, color one part red for the red stripes and dye the final part blue for the canton (background) on which the stars reside. You are now ready to create the American flag on your cake. When you have finished frosting it, fill a pastry bag with white icing to create the stars on the canton.

For a more healthful topping, use raspberries and blueberries for the red and blue parts of the flag. You can either fill in with white frosting, softened cream cheese or whipped cream.

Set the table with patriotic recyclable tableware and your patriotic flowerpots, and you are ready to celebrate the Fourth.

Decorating Yourself

Costumes for the Fourth of July are always appropriate, especially if you are marching in a parade. Most celebrants make a point of wearing only red, white and blue clothes, but if you want to go a step further, you and your kids can become American flags. You will need a navy blue sweatshirt and a pair of red sweat pants for each person. If sweat shirts and sweat pants are difficult to find in the summertime, use t-shirts and any kind of summer-weight red pants. Use white tape to make the requisite number of stripes on the red pants. Cut out stars from white adhesive paper and stick them to the blue shirts. Make a game of trying to get all 50 stars on each shirt. When everyone is dressed and decorated, take a photograph.

Resources

http://images.meredith.com/parents/pdf/flag.pdf

> This Website provides Fourth of July symbols that you can download for your kids to use as templates or to color.

http://familyfun.go.com/arts-and-crafts/season/minisite/4th-of-july-main/

> This Website contains lists of activities appropriate for the Fourth of July, including recipes.

The Star-Spangled Banner, (Yearling Books).

> Geared toward children between the ages of 4 and 6, this book illustrates the night of warfare that led to the birth of the national anthem.

Off to the Bike Path

Family bicycle rides can be high points in your summer plans. It is an activity in which every family member can participate, it is good exercise, it is a way to get to a destination and it is just plain fun. As long as you are properly equipped, you can plan a day's outing, a weekend trip or an extended vacation. Even if you or other family members prefer to drive on a vacation trip, you can take along your bikes (or maybe rent them) for day trips from a central location. The possibilities are unlimited.

The best way to determine if long family bike trips are feasible is to plan a day trip from home. Try to select a destination that takes you through a scenic or interesting route. If you have younger kids–ages 6 or 7–plan a short trip. Remember, you will have to ride home so do not use up everyone's energy riding to your destination. Save some for the trip home.

When you are ready to start, review the safety rules with your kids and be sure they know hand signals, traffic laws and rights-of-way. Check that everyone–including yourself–is wearing a helmet and layered clothes; for example, wear an extra sweater that can be pulled off or put back on depending on changes in the weather.

Plan to start early so that you will have time to relax at your destination. Give the kids time to play and explore. The bike ride itself is part of the fun, but an equally important factor is what you find to do along the way and at your destination.

Let the kids set your pace. This is not a race; you and the kids should agree that the point of the ride is to enjoy yourselves. Allow the time for distractions along the way; for example, you do not want to zoom past a mother duck leading her ducklings to a stream. As the old saying goes, take the time to smell the roses along the way.

Also, remember the legs of your younger children are not as long or as strong as yours. The kids are working hard to pump their bikes and may tire quickly. Carry along snacks and juice or water for breaks. And watch for signs of fatigue—you do not want to have to deal with a kid who is too tired to get himself or herself and the bike back home. Call for a break when you see signs of weariness in any of the children. You might consider having each child pack a small bag or backpack with snacks, water bottle, notebook, pencil and a disposable camera to carry and use when you stop for a rest. Later at home each child can add his own entry about the bike trip to the family activity album.

Bike Equipment

Kids develop both physically and mentally at different ages, so you must know your child in order to buy the right bike. Each child should use a bike that is safe for his age and physical dimensions. For instance, most 4- and 5-year-olds have the physical abilities to mount and balance a bike. However, a child under 6 should not ride alone in the street. You can make an exception to the rule if you think your kids are physically capable of riding along with you. Nevertheless, on a bike trip a parent or adult should ride in front of the kids as well as behind them.

Buying a Bike

Like buying clothes, always try on a bike for size. Unlike buying clothes, do not buy a bike that's too big, thinking the child will grow into it. An oversized bike can cause your child to lose control of it and possibly get hurt.

A bike is the right fit for a child when the child can sit on the seat with his feet flat on the ground and shoulders at the same level or lower than the handlebars. Children under age 7 should have bikes with coaster (foot) brakes, not hand brakes. However, children older than 7 can benefit from bikes with both coaster and hand brakes; they can get used to using hand brakes while still controlling their stops with the foot brakes.

Many parents remember buying bikes by wheel size. The rule of thumb for this is a 12-inch wheel for beginners, a 16-inch wheel for 5- to 7-year-olds, and a 20-inch wheel (with dual coaster and hand brakes) for kids up to age 10. Taller or older kids may require a 24-inch wheel, and growing teenagers may need a 26-inch wheel. These recommendations are subject, of course, to the sitting test in which the child sits on the bike seat to see if his feet are flat on the floor and shoulders are at handlebar level.

What about training wheels for beginning riders? Some parents believe they help; others feel they merely delay the child's learning to ride. If you decide to use them, remember they should be adjusted as your child's skills improve. Plus, the wobble in training wheels is supposed to be there–that is how your kids learn to balance.

Whatever size or style of bike you want to buy, be sure to have the rider take a test ride. Only then will you know if the bike is the right size and can be maneuvered safely by its rider.

Biking Gear for Very Young Children

If you have children too young to ride a bike, you have a few options. You can buy a frame-mounted seat for a toddler (a child over the age of 1-year). The seat fastens above your rear wheel so the child has a clearer view. However, you need to be aware that the child's extra weight increases braking time and affects your balance.

Your next options are trailer cycles and tandems. When your child outgrows a child seat, you can hitch a trailer to your bike. This is a low, mesh-covered seat that is supported by two wheels for stability. It rides far enough back from your bike wheel so that the spokes are out of reach, but the trailer is wider than your bike so you must be careful that one of its wheels do not slip off the side of the road. Be sure the trailer has a shoulder and seat harness and a flexible hitch that prevents the trailer from falling over if your bike falls.

A tandem trailer looks like a small bike with no front wheel. When you attach it to your bike, you have a temporary tandem bike or bicycle built for two. Some trailer cycles have working pedals and gears, but if your child does not know how to use these features correctly, you may have trouble maneuvering your bicycle.

Buying a Helmet

It is unacceptable to ride a bike without a safety helmet–three out of four bicycle accidents involve a head injury. Therefore, you want to outfit each child with a helmet that fits.

Kids' helmets are lightweight and comfortable and you want to buy those that are colorful and easily seen by motorists and other bicyclists. You also want to be sure to buy helmets that meet safety standards. Look on the inside of the helmet for a Consumer Product Safety Commission (CPSC) sticker, authorized by the U.S. government in 1999, or a Snell sticker, the approval seal of the Snell Memorial Foundation, which is a nonprofit organization that tests and sets strict standards.

Be sure the helmet sits level on your child's head; do not allow the child to wear a baseball cap or any other hat underneath it. The straps should fit snugly under the chin with no more than a finger's width of space between the chin and the strap.

The strap should always be fastened when riding. By the way, your kids can wear this same helmet when riding scooters or inline skating. However, helmets should never be worn while playing on a playground, since helmets and straps can get caught in playground equipment and choke a child.

Resources

www.bhsi.org/kidteach.htm

This Website lists bicycle safety rules for children. It should be a mandatory read for everyone who rides bikes.

www.bikemaine.org/parentsguide.htm

This Website is a parents' guide to buying bicycles for kids.

www.sesameworkshop.org/parents/solutions/information/article. php?contentId=29060&

This Website lists tips for buying bicycle helmets.

A Trip
to a Farm

A visit to a farm can be an exciting excursion for kids of all ages. City kids, especially, enjoy seeing another way of life. You have read books about farmers and farm animals to your kids, yet many urban kids may not understand the connection between what they eat and the farms they read about. For these kids a field trip to a farm can be an eye-opener.

During the summer, a farm is at its planting, growing and harvesting peak so your kids can see the role agriculture plays in everyday life. There are vegetable farms, fruit orchards, berry fields, flower farms and sheep and goat farms. If there is a farmer's market in your area during the summer months, ask individual farmers about farms that welcome visitors. You can also visit farms at other times of the year. At Halloween, you can visit pumpkin farms and at Christmas, you may be able to locate a Christmas tree farm where you and your family can cut down your own tree.

Farms that accept visitors are a segment of a new growing industry called agritourism. Agritourism combines agriculture with tourism and provides both farmers and tourists unique experiences. It is also a part of a movement called new ruralism, which is a response to the stresses of modern life, especially urban life. People want to return to a simpler, back-to-the-land life-style and they particularly want to introduce their children to their connection to the land. Farmers, on the other hand, view agritourism as a way to make money that will enable them to make a profit while continuing to farm. By adding fruit and vegetable stands and special tourist events to their business, they can often actually save the family farm in the face of increasing farming costs.

What this movement can mean for you is that there are growing opportunities to make visiting a farm a part of your summer program. It helps to plan the visit so that you can take advantage of the educational process while you visit the farm. Do some research ahead of time, online or at the library. Older kids can help out with the research, and younger kids can look for books and stories about farm life.

Try to anticipate your kids' questions so you can provide appropriate information about rural life and agriculture before you actually visit the farm. You and your kids may also want to write down questions that your kids can ask the farmer in person.

Tips

Provide the children with notebooks and writing tools and ask them to keep a journal of what they observe on their visit. Take a camera along as well to record your visit. You can either take photos with your own camera, or you can supply disposable cameras to the kids who are able to operate the equipment. The printed photos can illustrate each child's journal.

For a day trip, arrange for meals and snacks. Many farms offer snacks or sell products grown on the farm. Call ahead and find out if there are provisions for meals and water or fluids. If you learn you have to provide meals and drinks, take plenty of water in an insulated water bottle along with food that does not spoil in warm weather. Carry provisions to dispose of your own trash (like a small trash bag) and hand wipes or towels to wash hands before and after eating. And find out what kind of bathroom facilities will be available so that you will know if you should make a bathroom stop before you reach the farm.

Finally, before you set off, be sure each child has suitable clothing (usually long pants, shirts with long sleeves that can be rolled up, a sweater or jacket and a hat). Do not forget sunscreen, insect repellant, hand wipes and–most important of all–boots.

Planning Activities

If you would like to visit an agritourist farm with an ongoing program for visitors, be sure to ask about the program when you call. Some farms have scheduled activities such as tours, pony rides, games, story hours, hayrides and playtime with animals. Others may only offer do-it-yourself fruit picking or vegetable harvesting. Still others gear their activities to younger children, offering supervised play with animals and information kits with coloring books and junior farmer certificates. Your selection of a farm should depend on the ages of your children. Both you and your younger children will probably appreciate the more supervised programs while older kids will welcome a measure of independence.

Many families prefer those farms that are set up for overnight stays of a few days to a couple of weeks. In smaller operations the guests stay in the farmhouse with the family, but many of the larger farms feature family cabins, chalets, big dormitories or bunkhouses. There is plenty of opportunity for interaction with the farm family and other guests while still being able to retreat to the guest accommodations for rest and relaxation. Most of these farms are working farms and the guests are encouraged to help with the chores. Families with children of all ages enjoy these vacations; the adults and older kids pitch in and often become proficient at tending crops or feeding animals. Younger kids tag along and help out but are often satisfied playing with the kittens in the barn, gathering eggs or feeding baby animals. Most agritourist farmers agree that no matter what their guests do, all find the rural locale and new experiences both a restful and an exciting change of pace.

Do-It-Yourself Planning

If the farm you choose to visit does not have a specific program, you may want to structure your visit by planning some activities for your kids. Begin with a set of basic ground rules that your kids understand:

- The farm is someone's home and it must be respected as their home.
- The farmer has the final say in what is on- and off-limits.
- You must ask permission before you enter or walk into a space whether or not it is a building, a field, a garden, an animal pen or a shed.
- You must not litter or leave any trash you create behind.
- You must treat animals with respect and not feed them, pet them, yell at them or run after them.
- You must be courteous to people who are working there and not interfere with their jobs.

Ask the farmer ahead of time if your kids can pick fruits or vegetables. Sometimes kids can package vegetables for the farmer's trip to market later or cull out bruised or damaged items. Also ask if the farmer can show the kids how to feed animals and teach the kids about each animal's diet. Is there a beehive you could observe? A pond where you can look for fish or study insects? Can you use your visit as a real-life laboratory to reinforce nature activities you have already done with your kids–like studying bugs, going fishing or bird watching?

Try to arrange a lesson about soil and composting. If the farm has a compost pile, for example, ask if you can insert a stick in the compost so that the kids can feel the heat generated by the pile. This is also a good time to discuss decomposition and the cycle of nature.

Whatever you plan to do, be sure to check with the farmer before starting any activity. After all, you, too, have to follow the ground rules. Furthermore, you need his or her help to ensure that every activity, exploration, chore and lesson is done in the safest way possible. Remember, neither you nor your kids are as familiar with the environment as the farmer is. So enlist his help in enforcing safety procedures so the visit is enjoyable for all.

Finding Farms to Visit

Whether you want a day trip or a week-long farm vacation, investigate all your options before you make a final decision. Prepare a list of questions before contacting the farmer. In that way you will obtain consistent information from each place you call or write.

The Internet is a good place to start. Go to a search engine and enter the phrase: farm visit. The response will be a list of farms in various locales (see familyeducation.com in Resources at the end of the chapter, for example) with a description of their programs and amenities. Some Websites focus on individual states in the United States; others list farms by type of activity. Visit these sites and click on any links that will take you to additional sites. You can also search for the term agritourism for sources.

Check local and regional telephone directories as well as reference directories in the public library. Follow up with phone calls or letters asking your list of questions. During each call, ask for additional references or suggestions. Ask the librarian for ideas and visit the travel or vacation section for resources. Finally, search for brochures or Websites for regional chambers of commerce in those locations you would like to visit.

Resources

www.agritourismworld.com

This Website gives an overview of agritourism and places to visit.

www.farmstop.com/aboutagritourism.asp

This Website explores the new agritourism movement and lists the types of activities that you may provide as a farmer or encounter as a tourist on an agritourist visit.

www.kidshealth.org/parent/firstaid_safe/home/farm_safety.html

This Website outlines the types of dangers encountered on a farm and discusses safety precautions to prevent injuries and illness. The site emphasizes safety measures to take around machinery, animals and water.

http://life.familyeducation.com/vacations/family-travel/29469.html?

Visit this Website to find a list of specific farms that offer agritourist tours and vacations in various states of the United States.

Neighborhood Junior Olympics

One way to encourage your kids to be active is to give them an opportunity to interact with other kids in physical games and activities. While your kids may play with each other, after a time this may become boring. They need a fresh perspective on the situation–maybe some fresh faces. How about kicking off a Junior Olympics Day for your kids and any other children who want to participate? You can start with the kids in your neighborhood, invite classmates from your childrens' schools or even turn to your extended family–cousins, nieces, nephews or young-thinking adults.

Real Olympics have many events in which the very best athletes compete against each other for global prizes and awards. You, too, can set up a similar event, but geared toward your participants and your location. If you have a large yard, or if you have a neighbor with a large yard, you can set up the games at home. If you need more space, you can go to a park. Be sure to check with your local authority about the park; some parks require that you reserve time to use a section of the facility, especially on a weekend.

Next, consider your competitors. Are they of widely differing age levels? Are some of them natural athletes while others are naturally clumsy? Are they all familiar with the same games or sports?

What about your facilities and equipment? Will you have the space to manage several competitions at once? Do you have enough equipment (or can you have everyone contribute equipment) to play a variety of games? Will you need extra adults or at least teenagers to supervise and to keep everything running smoothly?

Once you evaluate your advantages (lots of space, adults to help and sufficient equipment) and disadvantages (wide age difference among kids, insufficient space for several games at once or inadequate equipment), you can begin to plan the day.

Planning the Events

First, remember that this is whatever you want it to be. You are free to plan it to accommodate your competitors, your facilities and your equipment. Of these three elements, the competitors are the most important. You want to include everyone, so design games in which everyone can participate. For example, when planning the site for a baseball game, draw two parallel lines about three feet apart and ask 2- and 3-year-olds to kick a ball from one line to the other. Older kids can practice pitching, catching and batting several feet away. Take the emphasis off of scoring and place it on doing one's best. To this end, do not try to plan specific, tangible awards or trophies; a mighty cheer at each accomplishment might be enough reward, especially for the younger kids.

If your space is small, set up a schedule for events occurring one at a time. That way, each event will have spectators as the participants wait for their turn to perform or compete. And you do not need regulation sports equipment. Ask everyone to share equipment, and you can toss in some wiffle balls and bats for the younger kids. Although the entire idea is to have a formalized series of events, this is an adaptable activity. Whatever seems appropriate, fun and safe should be included.

If you have the space, it might be a good idea to separate activities for younger kids from those for older kids. Preteens, for example, may want to play a game of baseball or shoot baskets for points. Meanwhile, younger children can play competitive hopscotch, who-can-draw-the-best-sidewalk-chalk picture or jump rope. Try a wiffle baseball game with four players and one base. Handicap the game to accommodate different age and ability levels. Keep track of what is going on and make changes as necessary.

Possible Junior Olympic Events

In addition to standard baseball, basketball and tag football contests, you can set up other activities that your Olympiads can enjoy. Here are a few ideas.

Sidewalk Hoop Shooters

For young kids who are too short or small to make hoop shots, you can set up a hoop shot game on a sidewalk or driveway. You will need sidewalk chalk, a bucket, sand or rocks and a tennis or small rubber ball. Designate a court based on the contestants' size and abilities and draw a line at either end of the court. Place a bucket half full of sand or rocks in the middle of each court line. Standing or kneeling behind their bucket, players bounce the ball so that it lands in the bucket on the opposite side of the court. Opponents try to intercept the ball before it reaches their bucket and then bounce it back into the bucket across the court for one point.

Encourage the kids to invent their own rules once they have played the game a few times. For example, they may win extra points if they can make the ball bounce several times, or dribble, before it lands in the other side's bucket.

Circling the Ball Around

Older kids may enjoy sharpening their skills while competing for points. In this event, create a large circle with jump ropes on a driveway or playground. Have the contestants dribble a basketball around and around the circle until they are at ease handling the ball. Gradually make the circle smaller and smaller in diameter while the players continue to dribble the ball. As the circle of ropes grows smaller, the players will be forced to improve their handling of the ball.

Circling the Bike Around

Using the same layout with the jump ropes, ask the contestants to ride their bikes around the circle as it becomes smaller. Again, this will test the players' ability to handle and balance their bikes. Do not forget to be sure the kids are wearing their bicycle helmets.

Swimming Contests

If you have access to a swimming pool, you can mark off distances and conduct races in the water. Or you can have the kids swim laps while you time them. If you do not have access to a pool, you can still conduct water races using containers of water.

Place two tubs filled with water next to each other. Assign a player to a tub and give him or her a cork. At the signal to go, each contestant blows his cork across the water in the tub to the other side. The player whose cork reaches the other side first is the winner.

You can also have a high dive contest without benefit of a swimming pool. Provide a cup of water, a chair and ten pennies to each team. A team member steps up on the chair and tries to toss the pennies into the team's cup of water below. The player who tosses the most pennies into the cup wins a point for his or her team.

Closing the Games

After a day of outdoor fun in the Olympics spirit, it is always fun to schedule a closing event. How about a picnic or party? If the Junior Olympics have been a joint effort, make the picnic a potluck. Or plan something very simple, like hot dogs, hamburgers, vegetable sticks and maybe cupcakes for dessert. After all of the activities occurring that day, you will want to have plenty of water and juices on hand. You do not have to feel that you must produce a full-blown party; you are just capping off the day with a simple meal and socializing. After the fresh air and exercise, the fun and socializing that happens over dinner can be an enjoyable way to get to know your neighbors, to relive a fun-filled day or—best of all—to schedule the next Junior Olympics Day.

Resources

www.growingkids.co.uk/AthleticsForKids.html

This Website discusses athletics for kids and offers tips about training with kids.

www.cyb.com

This Website offers links on kids' health topics pertaining to exercise and fitness.

Something Special for Grandma & Grandpa

49

Making something special for Grandma and Grandpa is one of the easiest summer projects you will have. Grandparents as a rule have built-in receptors that tune in to grandchildren very easily. Therefore, you know that whatever you make for grandparents or do with them will be enthusiastically received.

If you live in the same area as the grandparents or even in the same house, you can encourage your kids to spend time with Grandma and Grandpa. What they do together, of course, will depend on everyone's interests and capabilities.

Many grandparents enjoy taking grandchildren to the theater, concerts or other events that parents may not have the time to attend. Such trips expand the children's horizons and enable the grandparents to relive the event through the children's eyes. Why not turn the tables and invite the grandparents to events the children participate in? Ask Grandma to go on a nature walk. Or bird watching. The kids may be surprised at how much Grandma knows about birds. After all, bird watching may have never come up before. Maybe Grandpa can help plan a tree house or participate in a scavenger hunt. If the grandparents are not retired, they can go camping on the weekend with the family or make an excursion to a museum on Sunday afternoon.

Active grandparents can lead bike trips or teach a child how to swim. And what a fantastic source of traditional games. Ask Grandpa to teach everyone how to play kick the can. Or marbles. Encourage all of the grandparents to join you and the kids in your summer activities. They will add a new dimension to each event and allow your kids to see a new side of Grandma and Grandpa.

Grandparents as Resources

One of the most cherished feelings you can give to grandparents is the opportunity to connect the generations. Just think about what grandparents can contribute to such activities as building a family tree, trying family cookie recipes, learning new card games, reviving old-fashioned board games or teaching handiwork skills such as knitting or embroidery. Rather than sit on the sidelines, grandparents can jump in and pass on tips, skills and ideas to keep your kids interested and learning.

Family Tree

The best way to do this is to set up specific times when the kids can sit down and talk with their grandparents about what interests them, both the kids and the grandparents. Start with a family tree, for example. Help the kids develop a list of questions beyond the usual names of family members to ask their grandparents. Accompanied by a tape recorder or a skilled note-taker, the kids can ask questions such as the following:

- What was your childhood home like?
- What games did you play or what kinds of toys did you have when you were a child?
- Did you have a favorite toy?
- What was your favorite computer game? (This question will define the generations and the kids may find it hard to believe that Grandma and Grandpa did not have computers as kids.)
- Did you play with your brothers and sisters? (Note: many young kids will be surprised to learn that a older aunt was once a grandmother's sister–a good opportunity for the grandparent to explain family relationships.)
- What is your favorite memory when you were my age?
- Did you like school?
- What was your favorite subject?
- What did you do in school all day?
- What did you like to do on the weekends?

Personal questions like these will help your kids see their grandparents differently–more as children who were similar yet different from themselves. It will also allow the grandparents to learn what interests their grandchildren–again interests similar yet different from their own.

While the grandparents are talking about their past, you or your kids should also ask about other family members so that you can be certain that your family tree is as complete as it can be. This is a chance to explain family relationships to your kids and to talk about family names or anything else that sets your family apart from others.

Talents and Skills

In addition, this is the time to take advantage of any skills–known or unknown–

that grandparents can pass along to their grandchildren. For example, your kids may find out that Grandma was a champion fisherwoman in her day and took pride in her fishing skills. A perfect opportunity to set up a fishing date for her and the kids. Maybe she knitted while she waited for the fish to bite–another skill to pass on one-to-one. Did Grandpa play the guitar? Or the clarinet? Can he read music? Could he teach music to your kids? Do the grandparents have long-forgotten collections of coins or stamps? Can they play chess? The kids may find that each grandparent has many skills and talents to share and what better way to learn a new skill than from personal instruction.

Books

Many grandparents share a basic weakness: buying books for their grandchildren. What is usually different about these gifts is that the books may be favorites from the grandparents' childhoods. As a rule, these turn out to be classic books that kids of all ages like and this opens another door to an exchange of ideas between the generations. Grandparents will most likely love to read the books to the younger children and then talk about the story or pictures. It is interesting for you to eavesdrop to see how each participant relates to the book. Encourage your older kids, too, to share their perceptions of the books their grandparents suggest. You will learn a lot about your kids as well as their grandparents. This type of interaction may inspire you to add a reading day to your rainy day summer activities.

Grandchildren as Resources

Grandparents as resources are important to your kids. Yet grandchildren can also be vital resources for grandparents. This is one way you can teach your kids that giving is a two-way street.

Remembrances

Grandparents love to receive photos of their grandchildren. Any and all photos will do. Grandma and Grandpa will each need a formal brag portrait to carry in their wallets plus informal shots of everyday scenes. Therefore, when you and the kids takes pictures for the family activity album, include copies for the grandparents. If the grandparents live nearby, deliver the pictures personally and ask the kids to describe the activity photographed. If you mail the photos, send along a note from the kids telling about what was happening.

If you think you are bombarding the grandparents with too many photos, save a few and have the kids use them to construct a collage for the grandparents. Or enlarge especially good pictures and frame them. You can buy inexpensive frames at craft stores, and some come with mats. In fact, it is a good idea to keep some empty frames on hand for those perfect photos.

Giving Back

It is never too soon to teach your kids to reach out to help their grandparents. Even if the grandparents are active and busy, they will always appreciate help from a grandchild. Therefore, an ideal summer day activity when it is too hot or rainy to play outside is to construct a coupon book for Grandma and Grandpa. Your artistic kids can even illustrate it with their own drawings.

The key to a good coupon book is to have the kids offer services that bring the kids and grandparents together for a day or an afternoon. For example, suggest that the kids return some of the favors that Grandma and Grandpa have done. In exchange for teaching them to knit or play cards, the grandchildren could offer a coupon to help the grandparents download some music from their computer or install new software. In fact, for those grandparents whose computer skills are weak or who are nervous around computers, help from grandchildren is always appreciated. Many grandparents never realized the full benefits of email until their grandchildren patiently taught them how to use the feature.

Other grandparents may need a little help finishing chores around the house. Encourage your kids to offer coupons that will get the necessary job done but are at the same time unique. For instance, the kids could write a coupon that could be redeemed to wash all the windows in rooms that contain the letter r in their name, such as livingroom, dining room, sunroom and bedroom. Or help plant spring bulbs or rake leaves at the end of any summer that includes the month of August (a humorous coupon). Make the coupon writing fun, and the kids will enjoy making a game of finding just the right wording.

Resources

That's What Grandparents Are For, (Peel Publications, 2001).

> This book is a read-aloud poem describing the roles of a grandparent in a child's life.

Grandparents' Memory Book: Did You Really Walk Five Miles to School?, (Sta-Kris, 1997).

> This book contains pages to be filled in by a grandparent. The pages ask personal questions about the grandparents' life, likes and dislikes. A good start for a family history discussion between child and grandparent.

Stocking Up

Planning 50 things to do with your kids during the summer seems like a big job. Not only do you have to think of projects and activities, but also you have to obtain the supplies and equipment to carry out your plans. Granted, some ideas, such as teaching your kids to cook or going on a nature walk, only need time and ingenuity, but others require equipment, materials and specific items.

What can you do to meet your goals without spending a lot of time, money or energy in gathering supplies?

First, if you plan far enough ahead of time to know that you will need special supplies for an activity, ask your kids to help find the material you need. This could take the form of a necessary scavenger hunt. You might want to set a budget or a time limit for looking for something and you might decide to postpone the activity until you have what you need. In short, this becomes yet another project for you and the kids to do together.

Another way to engage your kids is to search through your home, garage and basement for objects that could be converted into craft projects or games. This will test both you and your kids' inventiveness. Plus you will have the material you need for a project without having to purchase anything. Also, searching through your home may yield some supplies that you know you need for a planned project. The point is, start at home to see what you have to work with.

Craft Supplies

Many of your craft projects can be accomplished by using what you find around the house. Plus, you should begin the practice of saving items that seem likely to be useful. For instance, any cardboard or Styrofoam™ packing material can always be reused. Small cartons–cardboard, metal or plastic–are also valuable. Large appliance cartons can be converted into playhouses. Plastic bubble wrap can be danced on. Old computer paper can become an artist's drawing surface. View everything you are about to discard as potentially useful in a different format.

Craft objects also may require paints, brushes, markers, crayons, glue, paste, stickers, tape, yarn, glitter, fabric, papers or foamboard. You will probably have to purchase these items, but you may be able to purchase them in quantity so that you can use them on several projects. If your neighborhood has a craft store, watch for sales so that you can buy at a discount. Some craft stores also issue coupons for a certain percentage off or two-for-one sales. Clip and use these coupons for some good savings.

Check your telephone book or go online to look for discount stores that specialize in school supplies. Some areas even have special supply stores where elementary and art teachers shop for their classes. These are the places to find scientific equipment and supplies for nature hikes and science experiments. Many of these stores will sell to the public; they just do not advertise to the public. Be on the alert for sales at office supply stores where you can often buy office goods at a good price. These stores are good sources for special photographic computer printout paper for printing those digital photos for the family album and other scrapbooks.

Fortunately, you can make many of your own craft supplies from materials you have at home. You can make your own papier-mâché solution or hand puppets with materials you have around the house. If you or a grandparent sew, knit or embroider, save any scraps from your own work to use for those crafts. Again, stop to evaluate any use you can possibly make of items you want to throw away.

Sports Equipment

There is no way around it: sports equipment is expensive. And it becomes even more expensive when you buy new equipment for a child to learn a new sport, only to have the child lose interest within a matter of weeks.

Unfortunately, that sometimes is the problem. Still, if your kids are interested in learning or advancing in a sport, equipment is important. If cost is an issue—or you suspect a child may lose interest in the sport—see if you can rent the equipment. Rental equipment can see you through the beginning until you can determine 1) if the child is truly interested in the sport or 2) if the child needs better or different equipment to reach his or her goals. It does not seem sensible to invest in expensive equipment until these two questions are answered.

If you cannot find rental equipment, ask around among friends and neighbors to see if you can borrow the equipment. Some families may have equipment packed away in their basement that their kids have outgrown. Hand-me-downs in good shape are an excellent solution. You might want to check your own basement or garage to see if you have some forgotten outgrown equipment that you could offer to another family.

Along these same lines, ask around to see if you can swap equipment. You will loan your son's hockey equipment in return for the use of a bicycle your neighbor's child has outgrown. You can plan to swap back when your child outgrows the bike and your neighbor's younger kid is tall enough to use it.

Borrowing and swapping, by the way, can apply to more than just sports equipment. Maybe your friend would be willing to loan out her portable sewing machine in return for use of your camping equipment. Or even swap kids for a day's activities. Playing with someone else's children every now and then may add interest to everyone's summer program.

Storage

So you decide to save everything you can think of on the chance that you may need it for a craft activity later. Or you begin to see sports equipment in different sizes for different children piling up in the vestibule. Too many bikes in the driveway? How do you store all of this stuff?

One suggestion is to start with medium-sized cartons. See if you can fit your craft supplies and equipment into one cardboard box with a good lid. You may have to store paints and other liquids in plastic bags inside the box. Can you fit the box onto a lower shelf of a bookcase or in a closet? This way the kids can reach it to get materials out and—more importantly—to put things away. If one box will not do, you may have to use two. Go to an office supply store and get collapsible boxes that have tight lids and handholds when they are put together.

Sports equipment is more difficult to store, simply because it is larger. If you have a basement or garage, you may want to erect metal shelves and assign a shelf to each child. It is also a good idea to give each kid a box so that all the smaller pieces of equipment can be confined to one area. A box also allows you to tote the equipment to a park if you plan a game away from home. If you live in an apartment building, see if there is an extra storage closet in the basement for you to use. Or maybe you will have to rely on the kindness of neighbors or friends.

Bicycles, of course, need to be locked, whether they are outside or inside. Be sure to purchase a sturdy tamper-free lock that your kids can operate. Combination locks are best, but the kids have to remember the combination. On the other hand, they have to remember the key for a key lock. Whichever you choose, be sure each child knows how to lock and unlock the bike. You may also want to use locks to secure boxes of equipment that are stored in public places.

A more perplexing storage problem, however, is finding a place to keep or display your kids' craft projects. Talk to your kids about setting aside some space in a family area to make a gallery to display their work. Some items will need shelves to rest on while others will need wall space. Try to find a place that can grow with the accumulation of projects and that can be a visible representation of the fun you have had all summer long.

Resources

The following Websites buy and sell used sports equipment that kids have outgrown:

www.playitagainsports.com/
www.sportxchange.com/
www.usedsports.com/

Smart, Friendly and Informative

The *50 plus one* series are thorough and detailed guides covering a wide range of topics–both personal and business related, supplying you, the reader, the information and resources you need and want in an easy-to-read format.

50 plus one

Ways to Improve Your Study Habits

by Stephen Edwards

Learn the importance of regular study time, create a study environment that is free of distractions and learn the importance of personal organization. Everyone who is trying to improve their academic standing needs help and this easy-to-use book with handy, practical tips is just the ticket.

6 x 9, paperback, 224 pgs. $14.95 U.S. $18.95 CAN
ISBN: 978-1-933766-08-9

50 plus one

Great Books You Should Have Read (and probably didn't)

by George Walsh

A masterpiece of information for individuals who want to expand their horizons or simply impress friends. Walsh and his advisory panel selected literary works, which have had the greatest impact on writing, government, international politics, religion and the arts & sciences. International in scope, the books chosen for this list have survived centuries and are considered essential for a liberal education.

6 x 9, paperback, 224 pgs. $14.95 U.S. $18.95 CAN
ISBN: 978-1-933766-08-9

50 plus one

Greatest Sports Heroes of All Times (North American Edition)

by Paul J. Christopher

Hold It! You really think we can come up with the greatest sports heroes of all time? Well, we can and we have! Our heroes cut across all sports and are not limited to the most popular spectator sports. On occasion our heroes go back several generations, not just the names in the papers or the sports talk shows.

6 x 9, paperback, 224 pgs. $14.95 U.S. $18.95 CAN
ISBN: 978-1-933766-09-6

50 plus one

Greatest Modern Heroes

by Lucas Otto

Who is a modern hero? Men and women who have influenced society, changed our views, sought to make the world a better place, entertained us and made us laugh and even gave their lives for their ideals and values. Without them our lives would be significantly different.

6 x 9, paperback, 224 pgs. $14.95 U.S. $18.95 CAN
ISBN: 978-1-933766-13-3